Grow it! Cook it!

The beginner's guide to producing your own food

Linda Gray

SPRING HILL

Published by Spring Hill

Spring Hill is an imprint of How To Books Ltd
Spring Hill House, Spring Hill Road,
Begbroke, Oxford, OX5 1RX, United Kingdom
Tel: (01865) 375794 Fax: (01865) 379162
info@howtobooks.co.uk
www.howtobooks.co.uk

How To Books greatly reduce the carbon footprint of their books by sourcing their typesetting and printing in the UK.

First edition 2009
Reprinted 2009
Second edition 2012

British Library Cataloguing in Publication Data
A catalogue record for this book is available from the British Library

ISBN: 978 1 905862 78 8

Produced for How To Books by Deer Park Productions, Tavistock
Illustrations by Rebecca Peacock
Typeset by TW Typesetting, Plymouth, Devon
Printed and bound in Great Britain by Bell & Bain Ltd, Glasgow

NOTE: The material contained in this book is set out in good faith for general guidance and no liability can be accepted for loss or expense incurred as a result of relying in particular circumstances on statements made in this book. Laws and regulations may be complex and liable to change, and readers should check the current position with the relevant authorities before making personal arrangements.

Grow it! Cook it!

CONTENTS

INTRODUCTION

Producing your own food and other household groceries is not only extremely rewarding but, in times of economic and environment changes, a must!

Gardening has, until recent years, been a way of life and a necessary commitment if families were to survive and grow. Nature provides everything the human body requires to survive, and cultivating some of those natural products in our own back garden will not only produce the best food on the planet for our loved ones, it is also economical and environmentally friendly.

Chemicals don't have to be used to produce perfectly shaped strawberries, petrol is not required to drive into your back garden to collect your food and, not only that, as you are exercising and getting a dose of fresh air every day, gym subscriptions and doctors visits will be a thing of the past.

Many crops can be produced in containers and in a relatively small space with a little pre-planning and organising. And many of these crops can be employed in different ways. Herbs are perfect for collecting brownie points for your culinary skills. They can also treat minor ailments and prevent colds and flu. Rather than getting a cold virus and passing it round and round the household, refuse to allow it into the house in the first place, by keeping healthy and strong. No more vitamin supplements or cold remedies to buy!

Grow It! Cook It! provides all the information you need to keep your family and friends healthy and enjoying life to the full. Gardening is more than a hobby, it's a way of life and needn't mean back ache and boring garden chores. Even without a garden, many plants can be grown in containers, on a balcony and indoors.

Get those wellies on and produce the best groceries in the world for your family and friends – and keep fit and healthy while you're doing it. *Grow It! Cook It!* will reduce your shopping bill, remove the supermarket stress, and take you and your family into a healthier future.

CHAPTER 1

THE SALAD BOWL

A bowl of mixed salad is one of the healthiest, easiest and tastiest meals you can prepare for you and your family. Kids don't always appreciate green leafy vegetables, but chopped lettuce stirred into a bowl of colourful peppers and tomatoes always goes down a treat!

Growing salad ingredients couldn't be easier and many can be grown indoors, in a conservatory or even a window box, as well as outside in a traditional garden. If you have a conservatory or greenhouse, salad can be grown almost all year round – although, as it's eaten raw and often cold, other veggies can be eaten during the cooler months of the year. Eating seasonally is a good rule of thumb when balancing a healthy diet.

This chapter covers five main ingredients of a nutritious and delicious salad bowl:

- tomatoes
- lettuce

- cucumber
- peppers
- onions.

There are many other vegetables you can add as and when you have them available:

- carrots – grated or finely sliced
- garlic – crushed or finely chopped
- *mange tout* – whole or cut in half
- fresh peas or beans – cooked and then cooled
- herbs and edible flowers
- nuts and seeds.

Prepare your salad as close to meal time as possible. As soon as you start cutting vegetables, they begin to lose some of their vitamin content. However, picking your salad from the garden in the afternoon and eating it in the evening is a lot better than buying tired, old looking vegetables from the supermarket.

If your little darlings refuse to eat anything that doesn't come out of a packet, you could try tipping the tomatoes into a freezer bag on the quiet and then make a big deal about getting them out of the fridge later. Or even better, get them involved in the garden.

TOMATOES

About tomatoes

There is evidence that the Incan civilisation grew tomatoes as a food crop but over the centuries the tomato was grown as an ornamental plant because the fruits were thought to be poisonous.

By the early nineteenth century the tomato was once again considered a worthy food crop and businessmen ate tomatoes in public places to prove the fruit was in fact edible and could be safely consumed. The earliest recorded tomato ketchup recipe was developed in 1818.

Because tomato plants are self-pollinating, they tend not to change the components of their particular variety very much, which means we have many heirloom varieties available today, as well as many new hybrids in all sorts of shapes and colours.

Properties of tomatoes

Recent scientific experiments indicate that tomatoes, especially cooked ones, can help eliminate free radicals from the body, so reducing the risk of certain cancers.

Tomatoes contain significant amounts of vitamins A, B1, B2, B6 and vitamin C. They also contain fibre and a medium-sized tomato will only add around 20 calories to your daily calorie count.

Tomatoes are one of the few fruits that retain their goodness when cooked and it has been shown that the body absorbs the vitamins more easily from cooked tomatoes.

Growing tomatoes

Growing tomatoes is fairly straightforward even if you have never grown veggies before. Take it step by step and you can't go wrong. Sometimes nature gets in the way, but there are a few ways to get around even the meanest of nature's tricks!

First choose the tomatoes you want to grow. There are so many different varieties, you could browse the seed catalogues for hours. Go for a couple of easy types if you've never done this before. Choose a regular everyday garden tomato and maybe a cherry variety.

The larger beefsteak tomatoes take a little longer to mature and can sometimes be difficult to ripen later on in the year. However, if you have a long growing season, or if you just feel a little adventurous, go for it. The smaller tomatoes are wonderful for snacking and mixing into the salad bowl. Choose a yellow plum shape or a tiny red one. The larger varieties are good for making sauces and soups but can still be used in salads and sandwiches.

Once you've decided on your seeds, you need to prepare some growing trays. Fill trays or pots with seed compost and make sure they are well drained. Plants don't like waterlogged soil. Sow seeds according to the instructions on your seed packet. Different varieties will have different growing needs.

Generally tomato seed should be started off in early spring and kept warm and watered. Keep warm in a greenhouse or conservatory, or simply on a sunny windowsill. As long as the compost is kept warm and moist, the seeds should germinate within a couple of weeks.

When your plants are a few inches (15–20 cm) tall, re-plant into individual pots. Make sure the pots are well drained and keep the soil moist. Keep them inside until all danger of frost has passed.

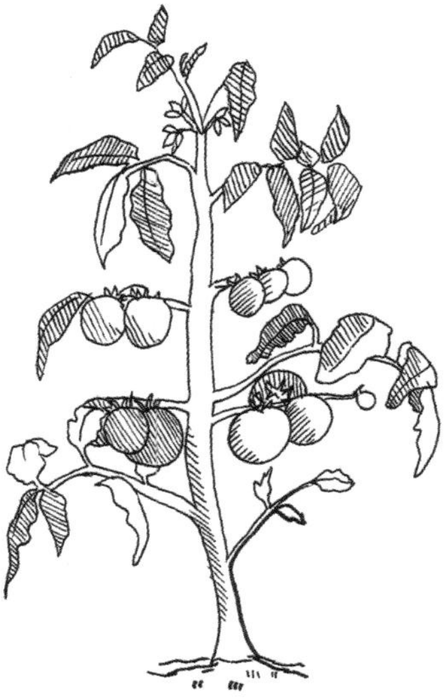

When the ground has warmed up, normally during May in the UK, put out the pots of tomatoes during the day and bring them in again at night for a few days. This will get them used to outside conditions.

As soon as all danger of frost has passed, plant them out in the garden. They should be about 12 in (30 cm) or more by now. Place a stake firmly in the ground for each plant before planting. Tie the plant gently tno the stake and water it well. Allow about 24 in (60 cm) between plants but check on your seed packet for variations.

It's also a good idea to scatter plants around the garden if you can. If a tomato plant gets blight or any other disease and is growing in a line with other tomato plants, the chances are you will lose the whole line. By scattering around the garden each plant will have more chance of avoiding the viruses.

If the weather gets a little cold, cover the plants in plastic at night to keep them warm. Use a cloche or a similar structure with clear plastic sheets. A cloche is like a miniature polytunnel and can be bought from most garden centres – or you could make one. Find some strong bendy poles, plastic or any other material will do, as long as it has a smooth surface. Push one end of the pole into the ground and bend it over to form an arch. Push the other end in and then repeat this process leaving around 12 in (30 cm) of space between each pole. Make sure the arch is high enough to accommodate your plants. When the line of arches is in place, throw over a sheet of clear plastic and hold it down along each long edge with bricks or logs. The bricks will stop the plastic from flying away, but should be easy enough to move when you need to access your plants. The plastic sheet must be long enough to fold down to the ground at each end to protect the plants from the cold at night.

Tomatoes can be grown successfully in pots and containers, however many varieties need support as they grow, so this should be taken into consideration when choosing the size and location of your container.

Containers must be well-drained and filled with fresh compost before planting. Compost dries out quicker in containers and as tomatoes need lots of water to thrive, they will probably need watering more regularly than plants growing in open ground. Never let your tomatoes go thirsty!

Keep your tomato plants free from weeds and water them regularly in dry weather. Never let them dry out. During the hot summer months, make sure you water your tomato plants every day, and look for signs of disease. Tomatoes can be fed with an organic fertilizer every couple of weeks during the growing period if necessary.

When your plants get a little bigger, they will start producing extra branches between the stem and the main branches. Pinch these out to encourage more fruit rather than foliage. Using your thumb and forefinger squeeze the bottom of the stems of the new branches and twist slightly to remove them from the main plant. A pair of garden scissors will do the job as well. Care should be taken not to damage the main plant.

Note that some people have allergies to tomato plants and gloves should be worn when pinching out the new growth. It's wise to wear gloves anyway to avoid staining your skin.

Once the plants have four or five bunches or 'sets' of fruit/flowers, pinch out the top of the plant to stop it producing any more sets. If the plant keeps producing new sets of fruits, many of the tomatoes may not fully ripen.

As soon as your tomatoes are fully ripe, pick and eat them! At the end of the season, pull up and compost the plants.

Eating tomatoes

Tomatoes are probably one of the most versatile foods available to us today. And the home grown tomato tastes like no other tomato can taste. Cooked tomatoes hold their vitamin content as well, which is even better!

SALADS

Sliced tomatoes are great mixed into the salad bowl or cut small cherry varieties in half. Chop a large tomato into very small pieces and stir the flesh and seeds of the tomato into a green salad. The tomato will act as a dressing.

Slice medium to large tomatoes on to a serving dish and sprinkle over a little chopped fennel or basil. Chill for half an hour before serving.

Chop spring onions or shallots and mix with chopped tomatoes. Garnish with a little finely chopped basil. Serve as a side dish.

Cooking with tomatoes

SAUCES

Use fresh tomatoes instead of tinned when making bolognese or chilli sauces. Choose tomatoes that are starting to go soft. Use in lasagne dishes, laying a few slices of a large tomato over the top of the dish when cooked. Grill for a couple of minutes before serving.

OMELETTE

Chop a tomato and mix with beaten eggs and grated cheese to make a tasty summer omelette. Garnish with a couple of slices of tomato and serve with a green salad.

Tomato Quiche

This is a great taste for those who love the egg and tomato combination!

Ingredients:

2 medium to large tomatoes, sliced
2 eggs
5 fl oz (150 ml) milk or single cream
4 oz (100 g) grated hard cheese
Seasoning
Bought or homemade pastry case

For baking blind you will need a sheet of greaseproof paper and some dried beans.

Homemade short-crust pastry ingredients:

6 oz (150 g) flour
3 oz (75 g) butter (or equivalent baking fat), cut into small cubes
Cold water

Method:

1. Pre-heat oven to gas mark 6 (400°F, 200°C).
2. Make the pastry by rubbing the cubes of butter gently into the flour until it resembles breadcrumbs. Then, adding a little cold water at a time, press the mixture together to form a dough. Add more flour if the mixture is a little sticky.
3. Roll out on a floured board and line a lightly greased ovenproof dish with the pastry.
4. Cover pastry with a layer of greaseproof paper and then a layer or two of dried beans. Bake in the pre-heated oven for 10–15 minutes until pastry is set.
5. Remove from the oven. Leave to cool slightly and remove beans and greaseproof paper. (Don't turn the oven off.)
6. Lay slices of tomato over the pastry base, keeping a few for the top.

7. Sprinkle over the grated cheese.
8. Beat eggs and milk in a bowl and add seasoning. Beat well then pour over the tomatoes and cheese.
9. Bake in the centre of oven for about 30 minutes until golden brown.
10. Arrange tomato slices over the top and grill under a medium heat for a few minutes. Serve hot or cold.

Stuffed Tomatoes

Use up leftovers to make this dish super-economical as well as fabulously tasty!

NB: When re-heating meat, always make sure it's piping hot right through before serving.

Ingredients:
4 large tomatoes
4 rashers of cooked bacon, chopped (or vegetarian substitute)
4 oz (100 g) finely sliced mushrooms
2–4 oz (50–100 g) grated cheese
1–2 oz (25–50 g) ground nuts
1 onion, finely chopped
A handful of fresh chopped herbs
A little cooking oil
Seasoning

Method:
1. Pre-heat oven to gas mark 4 (350°F, 180°C).
2. Slice the tops off the tomatoes. Gently scoop out the seeds and put to one side.
3. Place the tomatoes in a greased oven-proof dish.
4. Heat the cooking oil in a frying pan and cook the mushrooms and onions together for a few minutes, stirring to prevent burning.
5. Add the bacon, nuts, cheese, herbs and seasoning and mix well over a very low heat.

6. Remove from the heat. Stir in the set aside tomato seeds (optional) then carefully spoon the mixture into the four tomato shells.
7. Put the tops back on the tomatoes and bake in pre-heated oven for about 20 minutes or until hot right through.
8. Serve immediately with a green salad.

Tomato Soup

Ingredients:

As many tomatoes as your pan will hold
1 small–medium potato, peeled and diced
1 medium-sized onion, peeled and chopped
A little butter or cooking oil
A little chicken or vegetable stock
A handful of chopped fresh basil or any other seasonal herbs

Method:

1. In a fairly heavy-based large saucepan heat a little butter or cooking oil.
2. Gently cook diced potato and chopped onion, stirring gently with a wooden spoon until soft. Keep stirring to avoid sticking or burning. Remove from heat.
3. Peel and chop the tomatoes. TIP: To make peeling easier, put a few tomatoes at a time into a bowl and carefully pour boiling water over them. Leave for a few minutes then drain. Rub the skins off as soon as the tomatoes are cool enough to touch.
4. Add all the chopped peeled tomatoes to the pan with the potato and onion and stir. Add a little stock, or water if you haven't any stock available.
5. Stir over a low heat until the tomatoes are soft, adding a little stock or water if the mixture seems to be a little dry. Stir in some chopped basil or other herbs 5–10 minutes before the end of cooking time.
6. This soup can be liquidised if you prefer a smooth soup or eaten straight from the pan. After liquidising, re-heat over a very low heat, stirring for a few minutes until hot right through.
7. Serve with hot crusty bread.

HOUSEHOLD TIPS

- Tomatoes are a good deodoriser. To eliminate stale smells from the fridge, wipe undiluted tomato juice around the inside, then rinse and dry.
- Tomato juice can also be used to deodorise your dog after a smelly woodland walk. Sponge undiluted tomato juice all over your dog, avoiding his or her eyes, and wait a few minutes. Then shampoo or scrub with soap and water.
- For many years tomatoes have been used as 'weapons' during rural festivals!

LETTUCE

About lettuce

Lettuce is known to have been cultivated for thousands of years and was considered to represent good luck in China. The milky sap of cos lettuce was used in healing preparations by Roman physicians. Ancient wild varieties of lettuce contained a narcotic similar to opium and leaves were eaten after a meal to encourage sleep. The cultivated lettuce is said to originate from middle Europe.

There are many varieties of modern lettuce, including 'cut-and-come-again' types. These grow like small shrubs, and leaves can be cut from them every day. There are Italian red-tinged curly-leaved lettuces that grow well in a moderate climate, and of course the traditional British-style lettuce with its rich green tender leaves. When choosing your lettuce seed or plants, consider which varieties grow well in your region.

Properties of lettuce

Lettuce is a good source of vitamins A, C and folate, while being low in calories and high in water content. It is an excellent food for the slimmer and interesting enough even for the children!

The cos lettuce, also known as *romaine*, tends to be higher in vitamin and mineral content than other varieties. The 'rib' of the cos leaf can be a little bitter in taste, especially in a larger more mature lettuce. Although this part of the cos lettuce has been traditionally used in medicinal preparations, it can be cut out before the rest of the lettuce is added to your meal.

Growing lettuce

There are now many hybrid varieties of lettuce available for growing, and most will thrive in moderate climates. In hot dry weather, lettuce tends to 'bolt' or run to seed, so if you live in a region that enjoys long dry summers, choose a variety that will stand up to those conditions. Butterhead types are resistant to bolting and they come in a number of different varieties.

Get adventurous with lettuce. There are probably hundreds of different varieties you can grow. Try 'cut and come again' types. They grow like small bushes and you can cut from them every day during the height of the season. Also there are the cos type lettuces which are higher in vitamin content than most and will keep fresh for a few days in the fridge. Italian curly-leaved types are wonderful for adding colour and artistic flair to the salad bowl!

Look around in the garden centre local to you and choose varieties that seem to be popular in your area. Chances are they will probably grow well.

Start lettuce off early in the spring and keep seeds warm and watered until the weather is warm enough to put them outside. Fill well-drained seed trays with fresh new compost and sow a few seeds at a time.

Grow different types in each tray and put a marker in so you know what you've planted. When the small plants are large enough to handle they are ready to move. Transplant them carefully into another tray, individual pots or under a cloche outside if the ground is warm enough.

Lettuce seed usually has a high rate of germination and you will probably find you have more plants than you can cope with. The best way to grow lettuce is to plant a few seeds every few weeks throughout the summer months. Plant them directly outside in well prepared soil, after all danger of frost has passed. They are fast growing plants and can be used before they reach maturity if necessary.

Thin out the rows of seedlings and throw the discarded plants into the salad bowl or in a sandwich. Allow space for each plant to grow – check on the seed packets for spacing recommendations. Different types will have different needs. Thin out rows of seedlings when the ground is damp after rain, or water beforehand.

Keep your plants watered and weed free. If the weather is very dry and sunny, protect with a cover during the hottest part of the day.

Watch out for slugs and snails – lettuce are a feast for the slug family and they can devour a whole line of tender young plants in one evening. Protect the plants with organic slug repellents. Egg shells work well. Crush them and lay round each plant, making sure there are no gaps. The slug will find an entrance if there is one. Sharp sand or gravel can also help. Of course slugs won't go near salt but, as it will dissolve at the slightest hint of damp and then be absorbed by the soil, this isn't an ideal option.

Lettuce plants growing outside can also be attacked by birds. If you have a cat, you may not be troubled by birds, otherwise hang a line of old CD discs above the row of lettuce. That will put them off.

Birds can get easily tangled up in netting but you can buy very fine mesh netting to prevent any injury to wildlife.

Winter lettuce is a good crop to have in the garden. Some varieties may need protection under plastic or glass, but many will put up with very cold nights. Being high in water content though, it's unlikely they will survive a frost.

Grow a couple of plants in a greenhouse or conservatory to have a taste of summer throughout the winter months. Winter crop seeds should be planted in late summer or early autumn. Again check on the advice given on the seed packet.

Lettuces can also be grown in pots and containers outside or in the house. They are a useful indoor plant to grow along with herbs – especially for out-of-season months.

Always grow in well-drained pots of fresh compost, and water regularly. Lettuces grown in too much sun or with not enough water tend to bolt and become bitter in taste.

Eating lettuce

The best way to enjoy lettuce and keep it interesting at every meal is to grow as many different varieties as you can. Eating the same lettuce every day can be boring after a while, but with different colours, textures and tastes to choose from, the salad bowl will always be an exciting and tasty meal.

Lettuce is best eaten as fresh as possible and uncooked. Pick a few leaves from each plant in your garden early in the season and make an early spring salad. Remember to use the small lettuces you remove during thinning.

COLOURFUL SALAD

Mix lettuce types together to make a colourful salad bowl. There are lots of different greens and even red variegated lettuces that are easy to grow and delicious to eat.

MIXED SALAD

Finely shred lettuce leaves and mix into the salad bowl with chopped tomatoes, spring onions, peppers and anything else you have available. Stir in a few chopped nuts or sunflower seeds. Serve salad with all summer meals. Omelettes, quiche or chicken off the barbecue all taste better served with a tasty fresh green salad straight from the garden.

LETTUCE ADDITIVE

Chopped lettuce or whole lettuce leaves are a great addition to sandwiches or wraps. Fill a pitta bread with shredded lettuce and add cooked chicken slices or chopped boiled egg, with a little salad dressing or mayonnaise.

Cooking with lettuce

Coarse leaves from lettuces, such as cos, can be mixed with stir fry meals or added to rice or pasta dishes. Slice into thin ribbons and add to dishes during the final couple of minutes of cooking.

Lettuce Soup

Ingredients:

12 oz (350 g) chopped Cos lettuce leaves
4 oz (125 g) finely sliced spring onions or shallots
2 oz (50 g) butter or substitute

1 tablespoon (2 dessertspoons) flour
1 pint (½ litre) vegetable or chicken stock
¼ pint (150 mls) milk

Seasoning (a little salt and pepper or finely chopped herbs of your choice)

Method:
1. Gently heat butter in a large fairly heavy-based saucepan.
2. Add lettuce and onions to the pan and stir gently over a low heat until soft, being careful not to burn the vegetables.
3. Stir in the flour then add stock to the pan.
4. Bring to the boil, then reduce heat and simmer for about 20 minutes, stirring regularly. Remove from the heat and allow to cool for 5–10 minutes.
5. Liquidise soup in a blender or food processor until smooth.
   Return to the pan. Stir in milk and seasoning.
6. Re-heat over a low heat until piping hot right through, stirring all the time.
7. Serve hot with crusty bread or croutons.

CUCUMBER

About cucumber

There is evidence to suggest that the cucumber has been cultivated in western Asia for around 3,000 years. The Romans were very fond of the cucumber and cultivated it artificially to have it available for consumption all through the year. They were responsible for cucumber spreading across Europe although it took many centuries to reach all corners of Europe and America. By the sixteenth century, the cucumber was established throughout America and Europe.

In the late 1600s, all vegetables that were eaten uncooked were thought to bring on summer diseases and the cucumber therefore took a back seat in the vegetable garden for a couple of hundred years.

The cucumber is a squash and belongs to the same family of plants as pumpkins and gourds. There are many different varieties that can be grown in a mild climate, including some specially cultivated for pickling.

Properties of cucumber

The cucumber is very low in calories and has only a trace of fat making it one of the best diet foods available. One medium-sized cucumber will provide at least 25% of the recommended daily amount of vitamin C. Cucumbers also contain significant amounts of calcium, iron and potassium. They are a natural diuretic and it is also believed that they can help lower blood pressure.

Because they have a high cellulose content, cucumbers can be hard to digest if not chewed properly. People often complain that cucumbers give them indigestion but this can often be corrected with a little more chewing.

Growing cucumber

As the cucumber is originally a tropical plant, in some climates a little extra heat will be needed for the cucumbers to develop to full size. They are often grown in greenhouses or under cloches or cold frames. Where they grow best in your area will depend greatly on the length and temperature of your growing season.

In the UK many gardeners grow cucumbers in greenhouses and cold frames but, in a slightly warmer climate, all varieties can be successfully grown outside. A cold frame is a glass box with a lift-up lid, giving plants protection from cold draughts but still allowing full sun and rain from the top. Cold frames tend to be permanent structures and are a useful addition to the vegetable garden.

When you buy the seed, choose varieties which grow well in your region. The local garden centre should be able to tell you, or ask neighbours and local growers which types they have more success with. As more hybrids become available every year, there will probably be a suitable variety for growing outside in your region.

Start the seed in individual pots in a greenhouse or conservatory. Fill well-drained pots with fresh new compost and sow two seeds in each pot. If possible, buy or make biodegradable pots to start off your cucumber plants. When you transplant them, there will be less disturbance to the roots if you can plant the whole pot in the ground.

The cardboard insides from kitchen rolls or toilet rolls are useful for making biodegradable pots for very small plants. Cut them in half across the middle so you have two shorter tubes and put them directly on to a seed tray. Pots can also be made by rolling newspaper or other paper round a rolling pin two or three times, sliding the paper off and folding back one end to make a pot. They only have to stay together a short while and, if you fill a seed tray with pots, they hold each other up very well, especially when they are filled with compost. Otherwise, pot-making kits are readily available in garden centres.

If making your own pots isn't possible, you can still successfully re-plant the small plants but be careful not to handle them too much. Make sure the compost is damp before removing from the pot and ease the plant out gently, handling it as little as possible.

Plant out when the weather warms up and all danger of frost has passed. Allow a fairly large space for the plants to grow into. Check on your seed packet for growing recommendations, but they will normally need about 2–3 ft (60–90 cm) per plant all round.

Some growers use a ridge method where the plants are grown on a small hill of earth. Your seed packet may suggest this as the best way for your variety. Always check the growing recommendations before you start.

HOUSEHOLD TIPS

- Keep an eye out for slugs while your plants are small. Protect them with organic slug repellents. Crushed egg shells spread around plants deter slugs, and they withstand a little rain too.
- Try an old country method: slugs are attracted to beer and will drown in a bowl of beer rather than attack your baby plants – with a little luck. You will have to dispose of a bowl of dead drunk slugs in the morning though!

Keep the plants weed-free and watered. Pull weeds by hand rather than using a hoe. Young plants can be easily damaged by large tools. Cucumber plants trail over a fairly large area and, once grown, few weeds can battle through the undergrowth. Frogs and toads love the semi-tropical cover of cucumbers and other squash plants, and they will also keep slugs and snails to a minimum. Encourage frogs to your garden if you can.

Some varieties of cucumber will require male flowers to be removed, to avoid bitter tasting or poorly developed fruits. There are so many hybrid types available now that you will probably find one that doesn't need too much attention. There are also climbing varieties, useful where space is limited.

When the cucumber fruits start to grow, make sure they are not trailing on wet soil. Lift them gently on to a dry patch or lay straw underneath each one.

When the cucumber fruit can easily be twisted away from the stalk, it's ready to eat. With good conditions and a long warm summer, cucumbers can be very prolific. Be prepared to give some away!

There are smaller hybrid varieties that are suitable for container growing. Check on the manufacturer's growing recommendations on seed packets or plants before you buy.

Cucumber plants tend to grow over a large area so would need well-drained and very large pots to thrive. The compost should never be allowed to dry out completely.

Eating cucumber

Cucumber is generally eaten raw and fresh in salads and makes excellent sauces and dips to serve with hot dishes.

CUCUMBER DIP

Remove some, or all, of the peel from a cucumber. Chop the remaining flesh into fairly small pieces. The seeds can be discarded or left in according to taste and time available. Stir into a sauce made of half mayonnaise and half natural yoghurt, or a low fat *crème fraiche* mix.

Chilled Summer Soup

Make the most of your food processor with this quick and easy taste sensation!

Ingredients:

2 cucumbers
1 avocado

Chopped mint leaves to taste
Cream and mint leaves to garnish (optional)

Method:
1. Peel and chop the cucumbers, then mix with the flesh of the avocado.
2. Mix in chopped mint leaves to taste.
3. Blend in a food processor until smooth. Chill for about 30 minutes before serving.
4. Garnish with a swirl of cream and a couple of whole mint leaves.

SNACKS

Cucumber is a tasty aid to losing weight and makes an excellent snack. Cut into sticks and mix with carrot sticks and green or red pepper. Cucumber sticks are great for kids' lunchboxes and children love the fresh, slightly sweet taste.

SANDWICHES

For a healthy low calorie sandwich, spread cottage cheese, or any very low fat cheese, on to a slice of rye bread or low calorie crispbread. Finely slice a cucumber and pile as much as you can on to the cheese. The more you eat, the better for you.

Cucumber sandwiches have long been a favourite at elegant tea parties. Tiny triangular sandwiches without the crusts have been considered a food fit for royalty for many generations.

PICKLED CUCUMBER

There are a number of ways of pickling cucumber. A traditional method is to lay slices of peeled cucumber in a bowl and layer with salt. Leave it for 24 hours, then rinse and allow to dry a little. Put the salted cucumber into a jar with pickling vinegar. Seal the jar and leave it for about a month before using.

Quick Cucumber Pickle

This is a quick recipe that can be eaten the following day and kept for a few days in the fridge.

Ingredients:
Cucumber
White wine vinegar
1–2 teaspoons salt
A little bruised ginger (optional)

Method:
1. Wash and score down the length of the cucumber all round with a fork.
2. Cut into slices then sprinkle with salt. Leave for 10 minutes then rinse.
3. Put the sliced cucumber into a jar and pour white wine vinegar over to cover. Stir in a little ginger if liked.
4. Leave to marinate over night. Eat the following day or store in the fridge for a couple of days.

HOUSEHOLD TIPS

- The cucumber is a refreshing and cool vegetable and can reduce puffiness around the eyes. Lie back with a slice of cucumber over each closed eye for 15 minutes to get the full benefit.
- Slices of cucumber or cucumber juice can be gently dabbed on to sunburned skin to cool and soothe.

PEPPERS

About peppers

Peppers have been grown for thousands of years but they became more of an everyday food around the sixteenth century, especially in India and Europe.

There are many different types of pepper, but the two main species are chilli peppers and sweet peppers. It's fun to grow a few chilli pepper plants for those extra spicy dishes but sweet peppers are more versatile and both are relatively easy to grow. Sweet peppers are known as 'bell peppers' in many places. They can be used raw in salads and as a cooked vegetable.

Generally, sweet peppers are red, yellow or green. It can be difficult in a short growing season to produce healthy red or yellow peppers although, with a little greenhouse help, it's possible. Green peppers are easily cultivated and will produce many fruits in ideal conditions.

Properties of peppers

Peppers have a high vitamin content and are an excellent food for those convalescing after an illness. Mature red peppers have twice as much vitamin C as green peppers, so if you can grow a few it's worthwhile. Peppers aid a weight loss diet in as much as they are very low calorie and high vitamin foods. They help the body absorb calcium and iron, making them a good digestive aid as well. Weight for weight, peppers have a higher content of vitamins A and C than many other fruit and vegetables.

Chilli peppers are sometimes very hot, and should be eaten in moderation or not at all, depending on the delicacy of your stomach! Research indicates that hot spicy foods can increase the metabolism so they could be a healthy addition to a well-balanced diet.

Growing peppers

Sweet pepper seed can be started in late spring. It's very tempting to start them off early when there is a break in the weather, but peppers often become stunted and don't produce such a good harvest if they are started too early.

Prepare well-drained seed trays with fresh new compost and sow according to the recommendations on your seed packet. Generally, this will be in March or April. Keep the soil damp but never waterlogged. Peppers are a high water content vegetable and will rot quickly in very wet soil, but they shouldn't be allowed to dry out completely.

When your plants are large enough to handle, or when they have three or four true leaves, they can be transplanted into pots of fresh compost to grow on before they're put outside. Let them grow for another couple of weeks or so, keeping pots damp and warm. Don't put them outside before all danger of a frost has passed. Mid May is usually a safe time in the UK.

Choose a sunny spot, but not in the same soil that had potatoes or tomatoes growing during the previous year or so. Peppers belong to the same plant family and can pick up leftover bugs or viruses from the soil where tomato or potato plants have grown over the previous couple of years. If you are growing both sweet and chilli peppers, keep them as wide apart in the garden as possible to avoid cross-pollination.

Your plants will need about 12–18 in (30–45 cm) of all round space to grow, and should be gently transplanted, handling as little as possible. Protect them from slugs in the early stages of development. Slugs eat through the stem and can kill a whole line of peppers in one sitting.

Keep weeds away and water regularly, especially in hot dry weather. Although peppers enjoy a sunny spot in the garden, sometimes the midday sun can scorch the plants and dry them out too quickly. Watch out for this and be ready to protect the plants with some shade if necessary. Special sheets can be found at good garden centres that will protect your plants from the sun. Remember to remove the sheet as soon as plants are out of danger from the midday sun.

Pepper plants are often available in markets and garden centres in early spring. These plants were probably brought on inside or artificially, so they have to be acclimatised before putting out into the garden. Keep them indoors or in the greenhouse for a few weeks. They won't be frost hardy and probably won't survive a cold night.

Peppers can be grown indoors as house plants, although they should be placed in a very light place. If they are placed on a windowsill, make sure direct sunlight doesn't burn the leaves. They will need watering regularly, but never let pots become waterlogged.

If you are growing peppers in a greenhouse, polytunnel or under a cloche, they should be aired regularly. Gently loosen the soil around the stems to stop fungus or mould building up. Use a very small hand tool to avoid damaging the plants.

A healthy patch of pepper plants resembles a mini-rainforest and is an attractive feature in a vegetable garden. The plants will grow on quite late in the year, and can be protected from cold nights with a cloche.

As soon as the peppers can be twisted from the plant easily, they are ripe and ready to eat.

Peppers can also be grown in well-drained pots or containers on a patio or around the garden. Move the pots out of direct sunlight if they start drying out. Remember to move them back into the sun to allow the fruits to fully develop.

Well-drained pots and containers dry out quickly, so water regularly.

Eating peppers

Peppers are a versatile kitchen food and can be cooked as a vegetable or eaten raw. Green peppers tend to be crisper although the skin can be a little tougher than red or yellow peppers.

SNACKS

Peppers can be cut into strips and served with carrot and cucumber sticks as healthy snacks. Serve with a low fat garlic dip or a simple mayonnaise and plain yoghurt sauce.

SALADS

Thinly slice peppers into sticks or small cubes and mix into a chopped green salad. Cut into larger chunks to mix into a chunkier salad. Use a selection of colours if you have them available. Red and yellow peppers brighten up a green salad. Slice peppers into rings and lay on top of the salad as an edible garnish.

Cooking with peppers

Peppers can be cooked as a vegetable and can be added to many dishes to add bulk as well as nutrition.

STIR-FRIES

Cut peppers into fine strips and add to the pan a few minutes before serving to keep crisp, or add earlier during cooking if you prefer your peppers a little softer.

CHILLIES AND ONE-POT MEALS

Peppers can be added to many dishes including bolognese, chilli recipes and even traditional shepherd's pies and meat pies. They are also a good vegetable to add bulk to vegetarian dishes. Chop peppers and either simmer in a little boiling water for a few minutes before adding to the rest of the ingredients, or fry gently in a little oil.

Stuffed Peppers

This recipe uses sweet or 'bell' peppers. Any colour can be used, although green peppers tend to have a slightly coarser skin so may take a few minutes longer to cook than the yellow or orange varieties.

This is a handy recipe for using up leftovers.

Ingredients:
Peppers (allow 1–2 per person)
Cooked rice
Cooked minced beef, or vegetarian substitute
One or two finely chopped tomatoes
Chopped cooked onion
One or two cloves of garlic (chopped or crushed) according to taste
A teaspoon of fresh chopped herbs
A little grated cheese, or a slice of whatever cheese you have available

Method:
1. Pre-heat oven to gas mark 4 (350°F, 180°C).
2. Rinse peppers and slice the top off each one with a sharp knife. Put these 'lids' aside for the moment. Remove seeds from the insides of peppers.
3. In a bowl, mix cold rice with chopped tomato, chopped cooked onions, minced beef or vegetarian substitute and garlic and herbs. Stir ingredients together well.
4. Carefully spoon the mixture into the pepper cases and put the 'lids' on top.
5. Place on a non-stick baking tray, or add a little oil to the tray first to prevent peppers sticking or burning.

6. Bake in pre-heated oven for about half an hour or until peppers are tender and stuffing is hot right through.

NB: When re-heating meat, always make sure it's piping hot right through before serving.

7. Remove from the oven and take the tops off. Sprinkle a little grated cheese or other preferred cheese on top then grill under a medium heat until cheese melts. Serve hot with a salad.

ONIONS

About onions

Onions have, literally, been around just about forever. They have been cultivated for about 5,000 years and records indicate that they grew wild and were eaten in prehistoric times. There are many different types of onions you can grow, from tree onions to everyday ones. The choice is yours. If you have enough space, grow a few different varieties and have onions all year round.

The ancient Egyptians believed onions to have magical powers and they have been used for medicinal purposes for thousands of years. A common remedy for a dry cough is still used today and is very effective.

Properties of onions

Onions are one of the few vegetables that have been proved to help balance insulin levels. They can significantly help reduce cholesterol and the risk of heart disease. They are also a good source of vitamin C and B vitamins.

As well as being high in dietary fibre they are low in calories and a very versatile and tasty vegetable. Onions are a wholesome addition to a diet and can help ward off colds and flu symptoms as well as being essential in the kitchen.

Growing onions

Because of the vast range of onions you can grow, it would be impossible to cover them all here. There are many 'specialist' onions that originate from other than mild climates and these will need particular care. There should be manufacturer's growing recommendations with the seeds or 'sets' when you buy them.

To grow a regular crop of everyday kitchen onions, it's best to buy the seed in the form of bulbs or 'sets'. Garden centres stock these during the winter and early spring. It's possible to grow everyday onions from seed, but they do need extra care in the early stages and germination can take some time as well as being rather hit and miss.

Dig over the ground as soon as it is workable in spring and rake finely, removing any weeds and large stones. Plant the onion sets allowing about 6–8 in (15–20 cm) of growing room. Leave about 18 in (45 cm) between rows.

Pull out weeds as they appear and water regularly. The ground must be well drained. Onion sets will rot if left in waterlogged soil.

In hot dry weather onions sometimes run to seed or 'bolt'. If this happens, you will notice a woody stem growing straight up between the leaves. Break this off or bend it down if possible and let the plant grow on a little longer. Pick and use these onions. Onions that have run to seed have a hollow centre and will not store well.

When the onion leaves are dying back, bend over to the ground and leave for as long as the weather holds. On a sunny morning, pull the onions and lay on the dry soil for a day in the sun to dry out. Turn a few times during the day and keep them apart to allow air to circulate.

After your onions have dried out in the sun, plait them in strings or lay in dry wooden or cardboard boxes. Keep in a dry place out of direct light and they will keep for many months.

SPRING ONIONS

Spring onions should be started early in the spring in seedbeds or trays of fresh new compost. Sow seed *in situ*, preferably in a seedbed finely worked and clear of weeds and large stones. Check on your seed packet as some varieties germinate better by scattering the seed and raking it in gently rather than covering it.

When the onions are crowding in on each other, carefully thin them out. Make sure the ground is wet before thinning and gently lift out the weaker plants where possible, leaving a couple of inches of growing room for each onion. Use during the summer as required.

EVERLASTING ONIONS

Sometimes known as Welsh onions, everlasting onions literally will last 'forever'. They do need a certain amount of attention though. The best way to start your everlasting patch is to begin with a clump of onions either bought or donated from another grower in spring or autumn.

Separate the onions carefully, leaving as much root intact as possible and plant out in the spring or autumn, allowing about 2 ft (60 cm) of growing room for each plant. They look rather lonely with all this space when you first plant them out but, after a few months, they will be filling the gaps. Each bulb multiplies and will produce anything from 6 to 12 new onions.

Autumn plantings will be ready in the spring and come at a moment when there is little else available in the garden. Dig up a whole clump, use what you need in the kitchen and plant out a couple of strong rooted bulbs for autumn picking. Repeat with all the clumps. You can increase your patch by simply planting out more than you started with.

Use the everlasting onions or dig up and re-plant. If left too long, the plants will keep growing but the centre will begin to die back.

Onions are generally grown in open ground but with the right conditions, they should grow in containers or large pots. A trough-shaped container is a practical way of growing these kinds of crops.

Make sure all containers are well-drained. Use fresh compost and firm the compost down more than you would normally in a pot, as onions like to grow in fairly firm ground.

Water regularly and never let the compost or plants dry out.

Eating onions

No chef would be without onions, and a string of home grown organic onions hanging in the corner will inspire anyone to get imaginative in the kitchen. If you suffer with watering eyes when you are chopping onions, and the stronger the onion the worse it is, try cutting from the top of the onion and leaving the root end until last. Running water slowly over the onion helps, although this isn't easy to do while you are cutting them.

RAW ONIONS

Raw onions can be very strong in taste and aren't palatable for everyone. Spring onions, everlasting onions and other varieties of hybrid special onions are often milder and can be added to salads and eaten alone.

ONION AND TOMATO SALAD

Slice onions and tomatoes and sprinkle mixed herbs or chopped basil over the top. Chill for about 30 minutes before serving. Use shallots or milder onions if preferred.

PICKLED ONIONS

Pickling onions are slightly different from the regular kitchen onion, but they can be grown in the vegetable garden. Peel onions and put into sterilised jars. Pour pickling spiced vinegar over them to cover and seal the jars. Leave for a month or two before using.

GARNISH

Chopped spring onions, or ordinary onions if liked, can be used as a garnish on many meals as well as salad. Top cheese on toast with finely sliced spring onions or sprinkle on a cottage pie or omelette.

Cooking with onions

There aren't many dishes you can't add onions to, and the blandest meal will come alive with a little chopped onion added during cooking.

ONE-POT MEALS

Add chopped onions to the recipe early in the cooking time as they take a while to soften. Onions can be added to bolognese, chilli dishes, cottage pies and any other combination of mince-type meals you can produce. Onions bring out the flavour of mince.

Onions are also a wonderful addition to stews and casseroles, in slices or whole if they are small enough.

STIR-FRIES

Finely chopped or sliced onions can be added to almost any stir-fry meal, although they should be used in moderation as the onion will be less cooked and therefore stronger in taste.

BAKED ONION

Large onions can be baked and stuffed for an extra special addition to a Sunday roast. Peel the onion and carefully cut off about an inch from the top. Scoop out some of the inside and fill with cheese and a little chopped cooked bacon or vegetarian substitute. Bake in a medium oven until the onion is soft and the stuffing is piping hot right through.

Onion Soup

This soup can be made with any everyday onions or even shallots if available.

Ingredients:

2 lbs (900 g) onions, peeled and sliced
2 pints (1 litre) chicken or vegetable stock
1 tablespoon of flour
3 oz (75 g) butter
Seasoning

Cheese on toast or garlic flavoured croutons to serve (optional)

Method:

1. Gently heat butter in a heavy-based saucepan.
2. Add onions and cook over a low heat, stirring to prevent burning.
3. When onions are golden brown, stir in the flour. Mix well then add chicken or vegetable stock slowly. Stir to prevent lumps forming.

4. Add seasoning to taste and bring slowly to the boil, stirring regularly. Reduce heat and simmer for about 20 minutes.
5. Serve hot with triangles of cheese on toast or garlic-flavoured croutons.

NB: If you have trouble with lumps forming when you add flour, make a paste with the flour and a little stock before adding to the pan.

HOUSEHOLD TIPS

- Onions have been proven to alleviate coughs and other flu symptoms. Slice or chop an onion. Put into a bowl and sprinkle with a spoonful of sugar. Cover and leave overnight. The following morning, the liquid residue, which should be sipped, will soothe coughs and sore throats.
- Cut an onion in half and apply to a bee or wasp sting to reduce the swelling and relieve the soreness.
- It is also believed that if you eat a lot of onions, mosquitoes go in search of sweeter blood. This is probably where the warding off Dracula idea came from.

CHAPTER 2

DOWN TO ROOTS

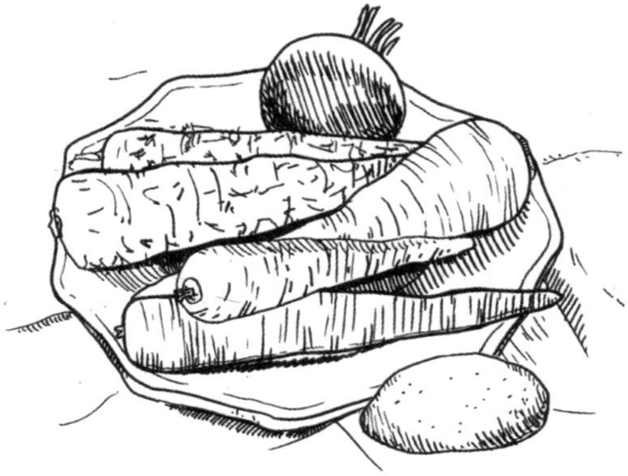

Root vegetables haven't always had a good image, probably because they are often covered in dirt and can be fairly dull in colour. But lurking beneath the somewhat unattractive exterior lies a world of nutrition waiting to be discovered.

This chapter covers five wholesome and nutritious root vegetables, all of which can be eaten as a separate vegetable or added to stews, casseroles, pickles and wines:

- carrots
- beetroot
- parsnips
- salsify
- potatoes.

Nearly all root vegetables can be added to stews, casseroles and curries. Most can be roasted and steamed and some can even be sautéed. Although salsify isn't a commonly found supermarket vegetable, it has traditionally been part of the kitchen garden for many years and is relatively easy to grow taking up little space and time.

Potatoes aren't truly a root vegetable but, as they live beneath the ground, we'll consider them roots for the moment. They are, botanically speaking, a tuber – a swelling from the root of the plant. Potatoes are a staple food and are probably one of the most wholesome vegetables we can grow in the garden. They can also be served hundreds of different ways!

Many root vegetables can be stored successfully for weeks, if not months, in a dry place out of light. Don't wash before storing. Dry and brush off excess soil then either place them in single layers in a cardboard or wooden box, in a barrel of sand or store in cloth sacks. Excess root vegetables can be pickled or made into wine.

There are some tasty recipes included for each root vegetable in this chapter proving they really are worth their weight in gold.

CARROTS

About carrots

We tend to think of carrots as long and slim, bright orange in colour and something you must eat if you want to see in the dark. Carrots are so much more than that though. There are many different varieties that will grow readily in the home garden, some with short fat roots, others long and slender. There are also other colours available.

Carrots have been cultivated for thousands of years and records indicate that different coloured carrots were grown, from black and purple through to reds and yellows. In Holland, in the mid sixteenth century, red and yellow carrots were crossed to create the orange variety we know so well today.

As well as being a wholesome and nutritious root vegetable, carrots have been used in medicinal preparations throughout the centuries. The Ancient Greeks believed them to be an effective aphrodisiac.

Properties of carrots

Carrots are reputed to help us see in the dark. This is probably due to the natural beta-carotene, a form of vitamin A. They also contain vitamins B1 and B6 and significant quantities of calcium and iron.

Carrots can be eaten raw or cooked and, because of their sweet flavour, are a vegetable that can be used in dishes such as carrot cake, as well as nourishing stews, casseroles and soups. Young children like the sweet taste of carrots and they should be encouraged to enjoy them. Get your children out into the garden with you and let them grow their own.

Growing carrots

Carrots, like all root vegetables, prefer a good depth of soil to develop fully. However, there are new varieties on the market that are shorter and fatter and these types should be chosen if you have shallow top soil in your garden.

Dig the soil over in the spring to a depth of about 12 in (30 cm) and remove large stones, non-organic debris and any perennial weeds. Mix in some well-rotted fertiliser or compost if the soil is a little tired. If possible, fertiliser should be incorporated into the soil during the previous autumn. Make sure whatever you dig in is well rotted though, or the carrots will fork, or split, and won't develop properly.

Check on your seed packet for growing recommendations, but generally carrot seed is started mid to late spring. Rake over the seed bed or vegetable patch to a fine tilth and sow very short lines of seed every couple of weeks or so right through until late summer if the weather is good enough. 'Tilth' is a word used for the cultivated soil prepared for crops. So a 'fine tilth' is crumbly soil like breadcrumbs, although not as fine!

There is a good reason for sowing short lines of carrot seed. When the plants are about 2–3 in tall (5 cm or more) they will need thinning and with a long line of carrot plants this can be a daunting task. Short lines take just a few minutes to thin out.

Carrots tend to be slow to germinate and you need to keep an eye on the area while you are waiting for them to start growing. Make sure the ground doesn't dry out or become waterlogged (carrot seed won't germinate at all in waterlogged ground). And keep weeds away. Carrot foliage is feathery, right from the start, so anything that doesn't look like a carrot plant should be pulled out. Pull weeds gently so as not to disturb the carrot seeds, and always by hand. A tool at this stage will damage the seeds.

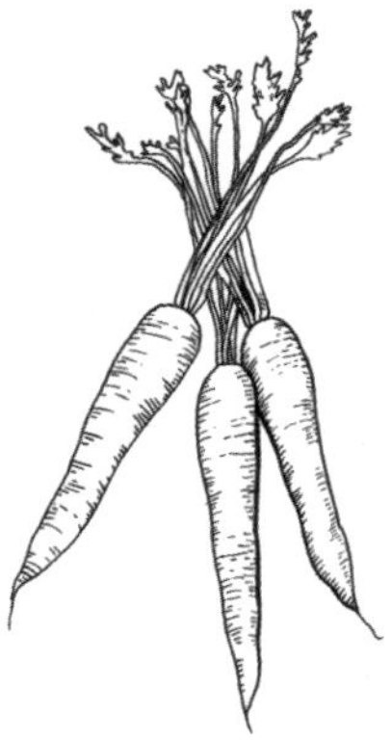

When your carrots are ready to thin, choose a damp day and make sure the soil is fairly wet before you start. The plants will pull out more easily and you won't disturb the ones you leave. Thin carrots by removing the weaker ones where possible and leave an inch between the plants for growth. After a couple of weeks, this whole process will need repeating and then again 2 or 3 weeks later, until each carrot has around 4 in (10 cm) to grow into. Double check on your seed packet as fatter varieties may need more space.

On the second and third thinnings, you will be pulling up tiny carrots. These can be eaten and are perfect for mixing into a salad bowl or adding bulk to a casserole or stew.

When your carrots are thinned, let them grow on until they are full size and pull them as you need them. Keep them watered in dry weather, and don't let them get bogged down with weeds.

Remember to plant a short line every couple of weeks or so to keep a constant supply going. Short lines of carrots can be planted in the herb bed or amongst the flowers if you are stretched for space. As long as they are not too shaded and get enough water they will grow just as well as if they were in the vegetable patch. If your plants don't grow well, it could be because the soil is depleted of minerals and needs feeding. Use an organic fertiliser to boost the productivity, but not fresh manure.

Generally carrots are considered to be a field crop and not suitable for growing in pots. Their long tap roots burrow deep into the soil and extract nutrients necessary for good development.

However, using short fat varieties in deep trough-like containers should work well. Always use well-drained containers of fresh compost. Water regularly and feed with an organic fertiliser from time to time. Double check on your seed packets for manufacturer's growing recommendations before you start, in case they specifically say 'unsuitable for container growing'.

Eating carrots

Carrots are a wonderfully adaptable vegetable in the kitchen. They can be eaten raw or cooked and can be added to sweet dishes as well as main meals.

SNACKS

Carrot sticks are a great way of adding colour and sweetness to, sometimes boring, 'healthy foods' especially where kids are concerned. Very young children shouldn't be given raw carrot as it takes a lot of chewing and there is a danger of choking. For older children, however, carrot sticks make a great packed lunch addition.

SALADS

Carrots can be added to just about any type of salad. They add colour and plenty of vitamins to the meal. The most difficult choice is how to cut them! Carrots can be sliced into rings; make them as thin as possible when adding to a salad bowl. They can be carefully cut into matchstick shapes or grated. Whatever the shape you decide on, carrots can be mixed into any green salad. Grated carrots also make an attractive garnish.

Cooking with carrots

Carrots can be steamed or boiled, stir-fried and even roasted. And of course they can be used to make the infamous carrot cake.

Carrot Cake

Because carrot cake is generally not on the same supermarket shelf as the cheaper cakes, we tend to think of it as being complicated to make at home. It isn't!

Ingredients:

For the cake:

8 oz (200 g) flour
2 teaspoons of baking powder
5 oz (125 g) sugar
4 carrots, prepared and grated
2 bananas, mashed
2 eggs, beaten
5 fl oz (125 ml) sunflower oil

Optional extras:

1–2 teaspoons of mixed spice or cinnamon to taste
Handful of raisins
2 oz (50 g) chopped walnuts

Cake topping:
2 oz (50 g) cream cheese
4 oz (100 g) icing sugar

Method:

1. Pre-heat oven to gas mark 4 (350°F, 180°C).
2. Beat all ingredients together well or use a food processor.
3. Pour into a lightly greased deep cake tin.
4. Bake for about an hour in the centre of the oven.
5. Remove and leave to cool on a wire rack.
6. Make topping by blending together cream cheese and icing sugar. Add a little more icing sugar for drier topping or a little more cream cheese for a softer topping. Spread over cake when completely cold.
7. Cake could then be decorated with walnut halves for a special finish.

BOILED BEEF AND CARROTS

Carrots and beef create a perfect combination of tastes. Always add a few carrot slices to beef casseroles and stews. Whole baby carrots can be used and have the sweetest flavour. Allow a little extra cooking time for whole carrots.

STIR-FRIES

Cut carrots into very fine sticks before adding to the pan. Cook for just a few minutes so that they keep their crunch.

ONE-POT MEALS

As well as stews and casseroles, carrots can be mixed into bolognese, chilli dishes, lasagne and shepherd's pies. Chop carrots into small pieces before adding to your recipe.

BEETROOT

About beetroot

Beetroot is believed to have originated from a sea plant that grew extensively over Europe and Asiatic coastlines. The root had been used in medicinal preparations for many centuries but not in the kitchen until around the seventeenth century. The leaves of beetroot were used as a green vegetable making the roots slow to develop into the globe shape we know today.

Beetroot leaves can be used like spinach, although removing too many leaves will stunt the root growth. Grow a few for the leaves and let the others develop into a healthy root.

The roots of beetroot were used in ancient times to treat many ailments, including fevers and constipation.

Properties of beetroot

Beetroot is packed with vitamins and minerals and has a high natural sugar content, making it an extremely useful food to include in a healthy well-balanced diet.

Beetroot is a good source of folate, vitamin C and dietary fibre, and the rich red pigment has been proven to fight against free radicals in the body. Beetroot is said to prolong life and probably does, with all the minerals and vitamins it contains.

It can be stored easily and is a good root vegetable to grow for pickling and using in the winter months.

Growing beetroot

Before you buy beetroot seed, check you have the right variety. Some beetroot is grown specifically for the leafy tops and others for the swollen globe-shaped root. The seeds bred for leafy growth probably won't produce fully mature roots.

Choose a fairly sunny position in the garden and dig over the ground to a depth of about 12 in (30 cm) or more. Beetroot will tolerate part shade but will need some sun and a light airy spot to thrive. The ground should be well drained with no chance of becoming waterlogged. Remove any large stones, non-organic debris and perennial weeds. Dig in some well-rotted manure in the season before planting, if necessary, and a little lime if your soil is very acidic. Don't add fresh manure or very rich compost just before planting, as this will cause the roots to fork.

Rake the ground over to a fine tilth and sow seed in late spring very sparsely along a row. Beetroot seeds are normally 'multiple' and will need thinning later on. One seed should be sown every couple of inches. They are fairly large and easy to handle although it's always best to handle seeds gently and as little as possible.

Once you have sown the seed, water well and keep free of weeds. When the seeds germinate they will produce small clumps of plants and the weaker ones should be removed. Wait until the ground is wet or water first before thinning plants. Gently remove the weaker plants leaving one every couple of inches to grow on. Firm the soil down around the plants you leave in the ground.

After two or three weeks it may be necessary to thin the plants again, eventually leaving around 6 in (15 cm) of space per plant. Double check on your seed packet as varieties differ. Larger beetroot varieties will need a larger space to grow into.

Watch out for birds when your plants are small. The red leaves are very attractive to birds and the plants may need netting until they become established. Use a bird-friendly net if needed.

Keep watered and free from weeds and loosen the soil gently around the stems of the plants from time to time. Use a small hand tool for this rather than a hoe. Beetroots grow close to the surface of the soil and a hoe could easily damage them.

Unless you have chosen a particularly large hybrid variety, beetroot should be harvested when they are about 3 in (7 or 8 cm) in diameter or they can become woody and lose some of their taste.

If you have a good crop, it's worth using a few when they are small. Tender young roots are nutritious and delicious and always worth a treat or two.

Harvest all beetroot before the first frost of winter. Twist off the tops rather than cutting them. This prevents the red pigment from 'bleeding'. Dry the roots but don't wash before storing. Beetroot can be stored for several days, and sometimes weeks, in a dark airy place. Beetroot is traditionally pickled for storing.

Beetroots are a root crop and generally grown in open ground. However, smaller varieties can be grown in fairly large containers quite successfully. Always make sure the containers are well-drained. Fill with a good seed compost before sowing seed. Water regularly.

Containers tend to dry out very quickly especially if they are in direct sun. Keep an eye on your plants for any signs of scorching from the sun or drying from lack of water.

Eating beetroot

Although beetroot is traditionally cooked and pickled, there are many other ways of serving this very wholesome and nutritious vegetable.

SALADS

Raw beetroot can be grated and added to salads. Peel first and grate finely. Stir into any mixed salad or use as a garnish for green salads or hard-boiled eggs.

Cooking with beetroot

Simmer beetroot with skins on until tender. Drain and cool. Remove the peel and cut into thin slices or dice. Serve with any dish as a cold vegetable, or eat while still warm. Cold, cooked beetroot is particularly good with salads, as well as boiled eggs.

Beetroot and Potato Salad

One great thing about beetroot is its colour. This recipe turns out pink enough to be irresistible!

Ingredients:

4 beetroots
4 potatoes
1 red onion, finely chopped or grated
1 small green pepper, finely chopped
¼ pint (150 mls) natural yoghurt
Parsley to garnish (optional)

Method:

1. Steam or boil beetroots until tender. Drain and leave to cool.
2. Peel potatoes (if necessary) and dice.
3. Steam or boil potatoes until just cooked. Drain and leave to cool.
4. Peel beetroots and chop into a large bowl.
5. Stir in the potatoes and onion and mix together well.
6. In a small bowl, mix finely chopped green pepper with natural yoghurt and stir into the potato and beetroot mixture. Save some to spoon over the salad before serving and garnish with parsley leaves.

PICKLED BEETROOT

Small beetroots are best for pickling mainly because they are easy to fit in jars. Find large sealable jars and wash before use. Place on their sides in a slow oven until dry.

Twist off the leaves of your beetroots and rinse. Place in a large pan and cover with water. Bring to the boil, then reduce heat and simmer until the beetroots are cooked. To check that they are cooked, carefully rub your thumb against the skin. If it starts to peel away easily, they should be ready. Drain and cool completely. Put into jars and pour over pickling vinegar. Seal the jars and label. Store in a cool place out of direct light.

Beetroot Soup

Ingredients:

6 small beetroots
2 stalks of celery
1–2 carrots
1 onion
1 parsnip
1–2 cloves garlic
2½ pints (1¼ litres) of chicken or vegetable stock
A little cooking oil

Method:

1. Chop onion and garlic and slice celery. Put into a large pan with a little cooking oil and water.
2. Cook gently for 4–5 minutes or until soft, stirring to prevent sticking.
3. Peel and grate parsnip, carrots and beetroots. Add to the pan with stock. Stir well.
4. Bring to the boil, then reduce the heat and simmer for 30–40 minutes or until all vegetables are cooked through. Serve hot.
5. Soup can be blended in a food processor if a smooth soup is preferred. Leave to cool for a couple of minutes, blend then return to the pan.
6. Over a very low heat, stir the soup gently to re-heat right through. Serve immediately with a swirl of single cream for an added touch of elegance.

PARSNIPS

About parsnips

Parsnips have been around for thousands of years and would grow wild over most of Europe if left to their own devices. They have always been a hardy and important root crop and were popular in Roman times as an everyday vegetable.

Because of their sweet flavour, parsnips have been used in sweet dishes as well as savoury. In medieval times they were added to bread recipes and also given to babies to soothe digestion. They are often still used to make wine and beer in rural areas.

Parsnips will re-seed themselves in a home garden and can become intrusive if not checked. They are easy to grow and will survive a mild winter. Parsnips taste even better after the first frost, when they contain more natural sugar and are sweeter to taste.

Properties of parsnips

Parsnips are closely related to the carrot, and very old recipes could have mistaken the two. They are higher in minerals and vitamin content than carrots, particularly in vitamin B5 (pantothenic acid). They are also a good source of dietary fibre and are rich in potassium. All in all, they are a very wholesome root vegetable.

Care should be taken if collecting wild parsnips as the plant is very similar to hemlock, which is poisonous.

Growing parsnips

To start your parsnips, it's best to buy seeds from a good supplier as germination can be erratic from seed collected from your own plants.

There are a number of different varieties of parsnip available. Some are short and some produce longer roots. If you have very shallow soil, choose a shorter type.

As with all root crops, parsnips will fork if planted in manure-rich soil. If the soil needs a boost, well-rotted compost or manure should be dug into the ground during the autumn before sowing.

Parsnips like a sunny position and should be positioned carefully in the garden as they are a long growing crop and will occupy space in the vegetable bed for a large part of the year.

Dig over the ground as deeply as you can and remove any large stones and perennial weeds. Rake over and sow seed directly outside. Parsnips won't transplant well so they should be sown *in situ.* Sow fairly thickly and handle the seed as little as possible. They should be sown in the spring, but check on the growing recommendations for your particular variety before sowing. Leave about 18–24 in (45–60 cm) between rows.

When the plants are a couple of inches (5 cm) high, thin them by pulling out the weaker ones and leaving one plant every inch or so to grow on. Do this when the ground is wet or water it first. Gently firm down the soil around the plants you leave to grow.

Thin again in a couple of weeks to allow about 4 in (10 cm) between plants. Fatter varieties may need slightly more space. Double-check the instructions on your seed packet. The small parsnips you pull out can be added to soups and stews to add bulk and loads of goodness.

Keep watered and weed free. Hoe gently from time to time, or loosen the ground with a hand trowel or fork to avoid damaging the roots.

As soon as the roots have developed, they can be eaten, probably not before late summer or early autumn though. Parsnips are known to taste better after the first frost of the year and many growers wait until then before harvesting them.

Parsnips can be stored for a few weeks in a cloth sack or laid in single layers in a cardboard or wooden box. Keep out of direct light and store in a dry, airy environment.

Leave a few plants in the ground to flower and produce seed for next year's planting. When the flower head starts to dry, place a cloth around the plants to collect the seed as it falls. Keep the seeds in a dry place until next spring. Otherwise, you can leave the seeds to fall and germinate where they land. They may not survive a very cold winter though. Collect a few and leave a few, but remember you will need to sow more seed from your own plants than you would if using hybrid seed.

Parsnips grow so well in open ground it hardly seems worth using pots or containers. However, if there's no other choice, choose shorter fatter varieties and treat as you would carrots grown in containers.

Always use well-drained pots and water regularly.

Eating parsnips

Parsnips are a lot more versatile than they first appear. There are a number of ways to eat them and all are worth trying.

STEAMED

Scrub (or peel non-organic) parsnips and rinse. Cut into slices and steam (or boil) for about 10 minutes or until tender. Drain and return to the pan. Add a knob of butter and some chopped fresh or dried herbs. Stir gently and serve hot.

ROASTED

Scrub or peel parsnips and cut them into large chunks or through the middle from top to tail. Either roast them around a joint of meat, or in their own pan with a little oil and mixed herbs if liked. Cook in a medium to hot oven for about 40 minutes or until cooked through. Turn over halfway through cooking. Parsnips can be dry roasted on a non-stick pan. Par boil for 5 minutes and drain well before laying them on the cooking tray.

Parsnip Soup

This recipe includes coriander, giving a mild curry flavour but it can be left out if preferred.

Ingredients:

2 lbs (900 g) parsnips, peeled or scrubbed and cut into small pieces
1 or 2 onions, peeled and chopped

2 oz (50 g) butter
1–2 tablespoons flour (or cornflour)
2 ½ pints (1 ¼ litres) of chicken or vegetable stock
Handful of chopped fresh coriander (optional)

Method:

1. Gently heat butter in a large pan and cook parsnips and onions for a few minutes. Stir to prevent burning.
2. Stir in flour, or make a paste with a little water before adding to the pan. It should be smooth to avoid lumps of flour forming in the soup.
3. Slowly add stock, then stir in the coriander if using.
4. Bring to the boil, then reduce heat and simmer for 45–50 minutes until vegetables are tender.
5. Remove from the heat and leave to cool for 10 minutes.
6. Blend in a liquidiser or food processor until smooth and return to the pan.
7. Heat through over a very low heat for a few minutes, stirring all the time. Serve hot, sprinkled with a garnish of finely chopped coriander, or other preferred herb.

PARSNIP SALAD

Very young parsnips can be lightly boiled or steamed, drained well and left to cool before adding to any salad.

PARSNIP SNACKS

Scrub or peel, and finely slice parsnips. Slice them with a peeler if possible to make them extra fine. Deep-fry the slices in hot oil for about three minutes. Drain on kitchen paper and then re-fry for another minute. Drain again and sprinkle with a little sea salt before serving.

SALSIFY

About salsify

Salsify isn't a vegetable we hear of much these days, and it is rarely available in supermarkets or grocers. Occasionally it can be found in local markets from late autumn through the winter months, but to be sure of a good supply of this wonderful hardy root crop, it's a good idea to grow it yourself.

Salsify is sometimes called 'oyster plant' as, when cooked, it has a slight taste of oysters. The root is similar to a long thin parsnip and can grow to 12 in or more. Salsify needs a good depth of soil to fully develop.

The plant produces an attractive flower and can be grown in borders and left in the ground right through the winter months.

Salsify has grown wild for thousands of years across Europe and up until the sixteenth century it was considered to be helpful in treating snakebites as well as diseases such as the plague. It wasn't cultivated until the Middle Ages and since then it has gone in and out of fashion in the kitchen garden.

Properties of salsify

Salsify contains many of the B vitamins as well as vitamins A and C. It also contains significant amounts of calcium, potassium and dietary fibre. It has no cholesterol or fat and is a nutritious winter vegetable. After the first frost the natural sugar increases in the root and salsify is said to be very good for diabetics because of the high levels of fructose (natural sugar).

The young leaves of the plant can be eaten in salads, although it's best not to strip too many leaves as you want the plant to put its energy into developing a strong healthy root rather than more foliage.

Growing salsify

Scorzonera is often grown in place of salsify. It is a similar crop in the same family of plants but has a stronger taste. It is also perennial so will re-seed itself and produce a permanent patch in the garden. Salsify, however, is an annual plant and will need to be planted every year.

The most important factor in growing salsify successfully is the depth of soil. Because of its hardiness it will probably grow just about anywhere in the garden. Try growing a short line in full sun and another in partial shade and compare the two. Salsify stays in the ground for a long time, right up until late autumn and in some cases can be left in the ground right through the winter months, making it a very useful winter crop in the kitchen garden.

Although the roots need depth of soil to fully develop, the plants don't take up much room in the vegetable bed and can be used as border plants to save space, or grown amongst the herbs or flowerbeds.

As soon as the ground is workable in early spring or late winter, dig over to a depth of 18 inches (45 cm) or more if possible. Remove any perennial weeds and large stones from the area and rake to a fine tilth. Salsify seed can be sown early in the year and will benefit from a frost or two in the early stages of its development.

Make a trench half an inch to an inch deep (1 or 2 cm). Sow seed thinly along the line and cover with fine soil. Check on your seed packet for variations before you start. Leave around 12 in (30 cm) between rows.

When the seeds have germinated and seedlings are a couple of inches high, they may need thinning depending on how thickly the seed was sown. Do this when the ground is wet. Water first if necessary. Pull out the weaker plants leaving about 8–12 in (20–30 cm) of growing room per plant. (Again, double-check on your seed packet for any variations.)

Water and keep the plants weed free. Salsify is a hardy plant and needs very little looking after once established. The plants are long growing and will stay in the ground right through until the following winter, and they rarely suffer from diseases or pest attacks. Use as soon as the roots have developed, generally from the beginning of autumn.

When digging up, loosen the soil around the plant with a fork, being careful not to damage the roots. You will need to dig deep if the soil has become compact. Don't pull the plants until you can feel they will come up easily, to avoid breaking the roots.

Salsify can be kept for a couple of days in the salad compartment of the fridge, but it's best to dig them up as you need them.

Salsify has a particularly long tap root and isn't usually grown in containers, although anything's possible!

Containers will need to be very deep and well-drained and replenished with fresh compost or fed with an organic fertiliser from time to time to allow the roots to develop well.

Eating salsify

Salsify can be boiled or mashed, added to cold dishes or eaten hot as a second vegetable. They can also be added to soups, stews, casseroles and curries.

BOILED OR STEAMED SALSIFY

Scrub thoroughly or peel salsify roots and cut into regular lengths. Steam or simmer gently until tender. Drain well and return to the pan with a little butter and chopped fresh herbs. Stir gently and serve hot.

ONE-POT MEALS

Scrub or peel roots and cut into lengths or slices. Add to casseroles, stews and curries as well as chilli and bolognese dishes to add bulk.

MASHED

Scrub roots, cut into lengths or slices and steam or simmer gently until soft. Drain well, then mash with a little butter and stir in a few chopped fresh herbs if liked.

Salsify Fritters

Add finely chopped onion before frying, or a handful of chopped fresh herbs to taste.

Ingredients:

1 lb (450 g) salsify roots, scrubbed and/or peeled
2 tablespoons thick cream
2 tablespoons Greek yoghurt
2 tablespoons cornflour
Seasoning
Vegetable oil

Method:

1. Cut prepared roots into lengths or slices and boil or steam for about 30 minutes, or until tender. Drain well and mash roughly.
2. Stir in cream, yoghurt, cornflour, seasoning and any herbs or onions you may be adding. Mix well together.
3. Heat vegetable oil in a frying pan and carefully drop teaspoons of the mixture into the hot oil.
4. Fry for a few minutes each side until golden brown.
5. Remove from heat and drain on kitchen paper.
6. Serve hot or cold.

Salsify and Eggs

This dish can taste different every time you make it – depending on the sauce you use. Match the sauce with the main meal for extra taste value.

Ingredients:

Salsify roots, scrubbed and/or peeled
Eggs, boiled and peeled
Sauce of your choice, options could include:
  Plain white béchamel sauce
  Cheese sauce
  Mushroom sauce
Chopped parsley or chives to garnish (optional)

Method:

1. Cut prepared salsify roots into chunky pieces and put into a pan. Cover with water.
2. Over a medium to high heat, bring to the boil. Reduce heat and simmer until tender.
3. Drain well and leave to cool.
4. When cooled, put into a bowl or serving dish and gently stir in chopped boiled eggs.
5. Serve immediately with a warm sauce poured over or chill for 10 minutes and serve without sauce.
6. Garnish with parsley or chopped chives.

POTATOES

About potatoes

Potatoes don't need any introduction as they have been a staple food of many countries for generations. In recent years, with diet fads and celebrity dress sizes, potatoes have had a bad 'carb' press. We do however need carbohydrates in a balanced diet and potatoes are perfect for that. Although they are a carbohydrate, they have a high mineral and vitamin content, unlike white bread or pasta.

Additives, such as oils and sauces add to the fat and calorie intake, but with fresh home grown potatoes, you won't want to add anything to spoil the perfect potato taste.

In generations past, people believed we could live on the humble spud alone, although the Irish potato famine brought home just how fragile that kind of dependence can be. Potatoes are an important part of our diet but shouldn't be eaten to the exclusion of everything else!

Properties of potatoes

As well as being a healthy carbohydrate, potatoes are a good source of vitamin C, B vitamins and minerals – lots of good reasons to include the potato in our everyday diets.

Potatoes have been used in medicinal preparations over many generations as a digestive aid, and also as a poultice for skin sores. The leaves, stems and fruits of the potato plant are poisonous and, because of this, potatoes have had a bad press in the past. However, the tubers (potatoes) that grow underground are a great source of wholesome goodness.

Growing potatoes

In days gone by, vegetable growers would plant just a piece of potato or even peelings to start another crop. This method does work but the plants are more susceptible to blight and other disease. The seed potatoes available in garden centres have been grown at high altitude and have a resistance to blight, although there is never any guarantee your plants won't suffer.

Blight tends to attack when the weather is warm and muggy. Some potato growers spray regularly with a 'Bordeaux' mix to prevent attacks. A Bordeaux mix is a combination of hydrated lime and copper sulphate and is available at most large garden centres.

Seed potatoes need to 'sprout' before planting. Place them in a box in single layers in a dark place until they have produced a sprout or two.

Early crop potatoes can be started before Christmas and should be ready to eat around Easter time. They will need protecting from the cold though and should be planted under cloches or in polytunnels.

Main crop potatoes should be planted around Easter time and will be fully developed by late summer.

Container growing

There are a number of different ways to grow potatoes and, with specially made containers on the market these days, you don't even need a vegetable patch to produce a good crop. Use a potato barrel and follow the recommendations that come with the container. Old rubber car tyres can be used as well. Some growers are concerned that the chemicals in the rubber may leak into the soil, but there doesn't seem to be any hard evidence of that so far.

Pile two or three tyres on top of each other and fill with fresh compost. Don't mix fresh fertiliser or manure into the soil. Plant seed potatoes about 6 in (15 cm) deep. Early potatoes can be grown in this way, as the tyres keep the soil warm enough for them to develop, although a plastic or glass cover should be placed across the top of the tyres to protect your plants during cold weather.

Traditionally potatoes have been grown in lines and 'earthed up' every couple of weeks (see overleaf). The best crop of potatoes will grow in well-prepared soil and, although this way of growing potatoes is labour intensive to begin with, you will get better results.

Potatoes and tomatoes shouldn't be planted near each other. They belong to the same family and will share diseases.

Choose a fairly sunny, well-drained spot and dig over the ground as deep as you can. Remove any non-organic debris, perennial weeds and large stones. Dig a trench to a depth of around 8 in (20 cm). Some varieties may need a little more depth. Check on the growing recommendations before you start for your particular variety. Tools can be bought or obtained for this job, although a simple spade will suffice.

When the seed potatoes have sprouted, lay them in the prepared trench allowing about 12 in (30 cm) between each one. Place them with the sprouts facing up as far as you can.

TIP: Comfrey leaves are a good tonic for the ground. If you have some available in the garden, lay the leaves in the trench and then place the seed potatoes on top of them.

Allow at least 2 ft (60 cm) between rows. Cover the potatoes with the soil you dug out to create the trench. Water well. Pull out any weeds that come up and keep the ground damp, but not waterlogged.

When the potato plants appear, they need 'earthing up' in order to keep the growing potatoes covered up – any exposed to the light will become green and inedible. Using a rake, carefully draw soil from both sides of each line to cover the new plants. Firm the soil on either side of the ridge and water. Repeat after a couple of weeks when the plants are beginning to show above the surface again. And then do it once more a few weeks later. After three times of earthing up your potatoes, you can leave them alone to get on with growing. Water well in dry periods and keep the weeds away, and you should get a good crop.

Steal a few new potatoes as a treat in the summer months. Use your hands to scrape away the earth from the sides of the ridge around the plants and choose a few baby potatoes. Push the soil back over the roots afterwards.

Use potatoes from the end of the summer or when the plants start dying back. Harvest the whole crop before autumn. If they are left in wet ground, potatoes will rot. Dig up every plant carefully using a fork, allowing a large area around each plant. Lay the potatoes on dry ground in the sun for a few hours. Turn over every now and again. Bring them in at night. If they are left too long in the sun they will become green and inedible, so just a few hours drying is enough.

Store in single layers in cardboard boxes or specially designed potato containers. Keep out of direct light in a dry place and they will last several months.

Eating potatoes

Potatoes are one of the most versatile vegetables on the planet. They can be used in so many ways it would be difficult to list them all in one book, let alone a chapter.

There are literally thousands of seed potatoes you can grow at home, although some varieties will be better suited to mash rather than roasts for example.

'Maris Piper' are a versatile all-rounder and are especially good for making chips. 'King Edwards' are a classic roast potato and are the traditional variety to serve at Christmas. 'Vivaldi' are perfect for boiling or mashing. To make a good choice of seed potato, it's best to scan online the varieties available (Thompson & Morgan have a great selection) or ask for advice at your local garden centre.

Potatoes from your own garden shouldn't need peeling, only very light scrubbing. Fresh potatoes out of the ground have very fine skins that can often be rubbed off easily. If the skin hasn't 'set', the potatoes aren't very suitable for 'jacket potatoes' but they can be used in every other way.

BOILED POTATOES

Prepare your potatoes as above and cut into fairly small pieces. Place in a pan and cover with water. Bring to the boil, then reduce heat and simmer until the potatoes are tender right through. They can also be steamed. Prepare in the same way and place in the steamer for around 20 minutes or until cooked. Drain well.

Once boiled, potatoes can be used in a variety of ways:

MASH

Mash boiled potatoes with a little butter and milk. Stir in a few chopped fresh herbs if liked. Mashed potatoes can be served hot with many everyday meals. Use to cover a mince and tomato dish to make a cottage or shepherd's pie.

Bubble and Squeak

This dish is an old English recipe traditionally using leftover veggies.

Ingredients:

Mashed potato
Finely chopped cooked greens (cabbage, spring greens or other green leafy vegetables as preferred)
Little milk or beaten egg

Oil for frying
Seasoning (optional)

Method:

1. In a fairly large bowl mix the mashed potato with finely chopped greens. Mix thoroughly and add seasoning if using.
2. If the mixture is a little dry, stir in some beaten egg or milk to bind together.
3. Form into burger shapes.
4. Heat oil in frying pan and gently cook burger shapes for a few minutes each side until golden brown, and hot right through.
5. Drain and serve hot.

Instead of mashing your boiled potatoes, they can be boiled and used in other ways:

POTATO SALAD

Cut prepared potatoes into regular-sized pieces and boil or steam until just cooked. Drain and leave to cool. When cold put the potato pieces into a bowl with a few chopped spring onions or shallots. Stir in a dressing made with half mayonnaise and half natural yoghurt, or use your preferred dressing. Chill before serving and garnish with a few chopped chives or a sprig of parsley.

Garlic Potatoes

A wholesome and delicious way of serving mid-week potatoes. Add a little finely chopped parsley to help keep the breath sweet!

Ingredients:

3 or 4 large potatoes, well scrubbed and peeled if necessary
2–3 cloves garlic, chopped or crushed
½–1 pint (300–600 mls) milk
2 oz (50 g) grated cheese
A little butter
Finely chopped parsley (optional)

Method:

1. Pre-heat oven to gas mark 5 (375°F, 190°C).
2. Cut prepared potatoes into ¼–½ inch slices and steam or boil until just cooked. Remove from heat and drain well. Don't overcook as the potatoes will be too mushy.
3. With the butter, grease a deep ovenproof dish.
4. Place the slices of cooked potato in layers in the dish dotting each layer with a little garlic. Sprinkle a little finely chopped parsley on each layer, if using.
5. Pour milk over until it reaches about halfway up the dish.
6. Cover with grated cheese and bake in the centre of the pre-heated oven for about 25–30 minutes.
7. Serve hot.

JACKET POTATOES

Choose medium to large potatoes with as few blemishes as possible. Scrub and bake in the oven until cooked through. Potatoes can be cut in half, sprinkled with grated cheese and browned under a grill. Or scoop out the flesh after cooking and mix in a bowl with tuna, cheese, ham, beans or whatever you have available. Mix the potato with your choice of filling and spoon mixture back into the skins. Put back into the oven to re-heat. If you are re-heating meat or fish make sure it is piping hot right through before serving.

ROAST POTATOES

Prepare and cut potatoes into fairly large pieces and boil for about 5 or 10 minutes. Drain and put on to an oven tray or around a Sunday roast. Cook for about 45 minutes to an hour, turning from time to time.

SNACKS

Potato skins can be sprinkled with a little sea salt and baked in a hot oven. Potatoes can also be cut and fried to make homemade chips or crisps, or baked as wedges.

There really are hundreds of ways to serve potatoes and using homegrown ones will make your meals even tastier.

HOUSEHOLD TIPS

Potatoes are not only versatile in the kitchen, they can also be utilised in a number of other areas around the house.

- Cut a potato in half and carve out a design to make a 'stamp' for the kids to paint with. Use thick poster paints for bright colours.
- Rub a raw potato over hands after cutting carrots or beetroots to help remove staining.
- Cut a raw potato into thick slices and arrange around a houseplant that has been suffering from worms in the roots. The worms are attracted to the potato, leaving your plant alone.
- Potatoes have also been used in the past as a cleaner for shoes, ornaments and various other household items. Rub the potato flesh over area and rinse afterwards.

CHAPTER 3

EVERYDAY VEG

Peas and beans have been traditional everyday vegetables for generations and they are easy to grow, eat and store.

Broccoli has had much media coverage over the last few years and is now known as a 'super-food'. It is also easy to grow and if you get it right, your plants will keep cropping for many months.

This chapter covers five main everyday vegetables that can be served with just about any meal:

- peas
- beans
- broccoli
- asparagus
- courgettes.

As well as being a 'second veg', all of these vegetables can be used as the main ingredient in particularly tasty dishes that ordinarily you may not consider everyday meals but are in fact just as simple as throwing a few fish fingers under the grill – well almost.

Although asparagus is usually considered to be a luxury vegetable, probably due to the price, it is in fact a great crop to grow in your garden. The benefits are enormous and as it's a perennial crop it comes back year after year. There isn't much maintenance involved either.

Courgettes have been grown in the UK for many years. We used to let them grow into full-sized marrows, but courgette hybrids these days will give a tasty crop of courgettes that you will want to eat before they swell into a rather bland marrow. Courgettes can be used in many dishes from ratatouille to a simple stir-fry.

All five of the everyday vegetables included in this chapter will grow successfully in a moderate climate with the right conditions and a little TLC.

PEAS

About peas

Peas have been cultivated for human consumption for thousands of years as a valuable dried food crop. It wasn't until a couple of hundred years ago that they were eaten as a fresh vegetable. Dried peas can be stored almost indefinitely, and were used on long sea voyages for crew and passengers alike where other foods perished.

As soon as the pea became a popular vegetable in the kitchen garden, cross-breeding began and nowadays we have many different varieties. The *mange tout* or sugar snap pea is eaten whole before the pea inside the pod starts to develop. These peas are excellent for snacks and salads. Then there are various sizes right through to the large 'marrowfat' types that are often used to make mushy peas and added to slow-cooked dishes.

Peas freeze well and with the relatively inexpensive frozen peas on the market, they have taken a back seat in the kitchen garden over the past 20 or 30 years. Although growing them yourself may not seem cost effective, they are a fun crop to grow and there is nothing like the taste of home produce. Children get involved in shelling peas quite happily and that in itself is a worthy reason to grow them yourself.

Properties of peas

Peas are a good source of vitamins A and C, both of which help neutralise free radicals. There is some evidence to support the fact that peas can help alleviate symptoms of age-related ailments. They contain B vitamins which boost the immune system and help keep the body strong and resistant to disease. They also contain significant amounts of niacin (vitamin B3), which helps the body to absorb iron.

Growing peas

Growing peas isn't a difficult process but it's worth arming yourself with the right information and equipment before you get started. Peas are normally a climbing plant, although you may find a hybrid variety that will grow as a small shrub. To support your climbing plants you will need some sort of trellis or fencing.

If your garden fence is facing south and gets a lot of sun, use the fence as a support. Attach a few strings horizontally every 6 in (15 cm) or so, and help the plants along by curling them round the strings as they grow. Pea plants send out tendrils, which enable them to cling on ferociously. Peas will happily use anything as a support frame, so keep an eye on surrounding plants.

They can also be grown along borders, although they will need support. Chicken wire or pig wire stretched across an area between posts is a good system. Make sure the posts or wire don't blow down in the wind. Pea netting is available from garden centres.

For shorter growing plants, pea sticks can be used successfully. Collect fairly straight branches from trees with a branch or two leading off each one for the plants to cling to. Last year's raspberry canes are very usable if tree branches aren't easy to find. Alternatively, buy pea supports from a garden centre.

Choose a sunny and well-drained spot in the garden. Although peas are a cool growing crop, they will need all the light they can get in the early stages of development, and again when the fruits mature. Peas and beans grow well together and, if you have the space, a 'pea and bean' patch is ideal.

As soon as the ground is workable in early spring, dig over and remove any perennial weeds, non-organic debris and large stones. Peas are usually planted early in the year as they are a cool growing crop. Check your seed packet for the manufacturer's growing recommendations for your particular variety. If possible, work the ground in the previous autumn and cover with an organic mulch. Dig over lightly before planting peas in late winter or early spring.

Once preparations are made for your pea patch, it's time to sow the seed. The seed you are planting is simply a dried pea. They are easy to handle and can be sown every couple of inches along a row.

Sow as close as possible to the pea support system you have in place. Make a trench about 1.5–2 in (3–5 cm) deep and place one pea seed every 2 in (5 cm) along the row. Cover the seeds with soil and water gently. Allow enough space between rows to maintain and harvest your crops.

Some growers prefer to soak seed in water for a few hours before sowing to encourage faster germination and, in days gone past, gardeners in rural areas would soak seed in paraffin to deter birds and mice. If birds or mice are a problem in your garden, cover with a wildlife-friendly netting until the seeds germinate.

Peas should come up within a couple of weeks and, all being well, will get on with the business of growing all by themselves. Water your plants if the ground is dry but never over water. Because peas are an early crop, they will normally get enough water from the natural rainfall.

In good conditions you can almost watch pea plants grow. When they first start growing they may need a little help to find the support system. Gently ease the tendrils round the sticks or netting.

From the flowers the fruits – pods – are produced. If you are growing sugar snap or *mange tout* varieties, pick as soon as the pods are a couple of inches long. They are sweet and tender at this size and become too coarse if left too long.

Everyday garden peas should be picked when there are obviously developed peas in the pods. Larger marrowfat peas will take longer to mature.

Peas can be left to dry on the plants and can be collected for using in the winter months, or for sowing the following year. Make sure peas are completely dry before storing. Keep in jars in a dry place out of direct light until required.

When your plants have died back, leave them in the ground until they have completely shrivelled and then dig into the soil. Pea plants capture nitrogen from the air and store it in their root system. Digging the plants back into the soil will replenish nitrogen and benefit next year's crops.

Because pea plants generally climb and need support, they are usually grown in open ground with a support structure of some kind. However, there doesn't seem to be any other reason why peas shouldn't grow in fairly large containers positioned against a fence or other support.

Check on the growing recommendations on your seed packet when you buy them. New hybrids are appearing all the time, and there may be a variety specially designed for container growing. Otherwise, choose a variety to suit your space.

Pots and containers must be well-drained and should be watered regularly.

Eating peas

Peas have been a valuable dried food crop for many generations and they are a perfect store cupboard ingredient for the winter months.

SALADS AND COLD DISHES

Sugar snap or *mange tout* peas can be added whole or chopped into salads. The sweet flavour is perfect with a chopped green salad. These varieties of peas are also great snacks for children. Serve them as a side dish tossed lightly in olive oil or a walnut salad dressing for a special treat.

Cooking with peas

FRESH GARDEN PEAS

Shell peas and boil or steam until tender. Drain and toss in a little melted butter and chopped mint. Serve hot.

MUSHY PEAS

Mushy peas are very popular in many parts of the UK, particularly the north of England. Made from large marrowfat peas, the recipe is simple to make at home. In a large heavy-based saucepan, cover marrowfat peas with water and bring to the boil. Add a little salt and sugar if liked. Reduce the heat and simmer until peas are soft and 'mushy'. Chopped mint or other fresh herbs can be added to spice up the flavour. Drain peas and mash until smooth. Serve hot.

CASSEROLES AND STEWS

Peas can be added to casseroles and stews. Fresh peas take a little longer to cook than bought frozen peas and should be added to your recipe at least 20 minutes before the end of cooking time.

Pea Soup

Pea soup has been a staple food in many parts of the UK for centuries. It was often left bubbling away on the stove for days, with ingredients added as and when available.

Ingredients:

2 lbs (900 g) shelled peas
1 onion, finely chopped
2 oz (50 g) butter
2 pints (1.1 litres) vegetable or chicken stock
A handful of chopped fresh mint
Seasoning

Method:

1. In a large saucepan, gently melt the butter over a low heat.
2. Add the chopped onion and cook until soft, stirring all the time to prevent sticking or burning.
3. Add the stock, peas, mint and seasoning. Stir and bring to the boil over a medium heat.

4. Reduce heat and simmer for 30–40 minutes, until peas are tender.
5. Remove from the heat and allow to cool for a couple of minutes.
6. Blend in a liquidiser or food processor until smooth.
7. Return to the pan and re-heat gently for a few minutes, stirring all the time.
8. Serve hot.

Pea Guacamole

Peas are used instead of avocado in this tasty variation of guacamole.

Ingredients:
12 oz (350 g) shelled peas
2 chopped spring onions (or use a shallot if preferred)
1–2 cloves of garlic
Juice of 1 lime (or half a lemon)
1 teaspoon of grated lime peel (or lemon if preferred)
1 tablespoon of olive oil
A handful of chopped fresh coriander
Seasoning

Method:
1. Steam or boil the peas until tender. Drain well and leave to cool right through.
2. When peas are cooled, put them into a food processor or liquidiser with all the other ingredients and blend until smooth.
3. Transfer to a serving dish and chill for 30 minutes before serving.

BEANS

About beans

Beans have been cultivated for home use since around the sixteenth century although it wasn't until the turn of the twentieth century that 'stringless' varieties were available to the home gardener. French beans, or bush beans, grow quickly and produce good crops without too much trouble.

Beans are best eaten whole before the bean inside the pod develops, although some can be left to mature and stored for winter use or sown the following year.

There are literally hundreds of different beans available for the home gardener to grow, although the basic French bean and runner bean are the most popular varieties and tend to crop well.

Properties of beans

Beans are a good source of vitamins A and C and can be safely eaten every day, but should always be cooked before consumption. Raw beans contain hydrocyanic acid, which is poisonous and can cause sickness and blood pressure problems. Once cooked, however, green beans can help reduce high blood pressure.

All green beans contain significant amounts of calcium and dietary fibre as well as folate and protein. The water in which beans are cooked will contain iron and should be used to make gravy or sauces rather than being discarded.

Growing beans

There are hundreds of different types of beans and, if you have the space, it's worthwhile experimenting with a few different varieties. French or bush beans take up little space in the garden and can be grown as a border plant. They are quick to grow and can be planted at regular intervals throughout the spring and summer months. Climbing varieties, such as runner beans need a little more attention but the taste is definitely worth the extra effort.

Generally beans need a sunny spot to develop well, although different varieties have different growing needs and it's best to check the manufacturer's growing recommendations before you decide on the right place. Peas and beans grow well together.

In a well-drained and sunny spot, dig the ground over and remove any perennial weeds, non-organic debris and large stones. Rake over to level the ground.

If you are planting climbing beans such as runner beans, they will need a support system to climb up. Many gardeners use a tepee method. Firmly place canes (6–8 ft long) into the ground in a circle and tie the tops together with garden twine to form a tepee shape. Run strings around the outside of the canes at 8–12 in (20–30 cm) intervals, wrapping twine around the canes to keep them in place. Alternatively a simple chicken or pig wire structure can be used.

Always make sure the support structure is firmly pushed into the ground to avoid damage in high winds. If the structure blows down, the plants will suffer.

Beans can be planted directly outside in late spring, after all danger of frost has passed. They are a fast growing plant and won't need an early start in the greenhouse.

Make a shallow trench (about an inch deep) as close as possible to the support you have in place. Plant your beans around the outside of the circle if you are using the tepee method and place individual beans every 2–3 in (5–6 cm). Cover with soil and water well. Sow French beans in lines, allowing 6–12 in (15–30 cm) between plants. Check on your seed packet for variations.

Beans love water but should never be allowed to become waterlogged. In hot dry periods, runner bean flowers should be 'set' by spraying with water at least once a day, preferably twice, or the flowers will drop off the plant and the beans won't develop.

Keep watered and weed-free, and your beans should grow well. As soon as you spot the young beans, start picking and eating, especially with French bean varieties. They crop well and it will be hard to keep up with them. Pick them and give some away or freeze for the winter months. A few may be left on the plants for planting next year. Decide on a few early beans to leave as they take a long time to reach full maturity. Store in a dark dry place for planting the following year.

When the plants have finished cropping, pull up and compost. Excess beans should be frozen quickly. They freeze well, but some of the texture and a little of the taste will be lost in freezing. Green beans will keep for a few days in the fridge after picking.

As with peas, beans often need a support structure to grow, and can be impractical for growing in containers. However, the small bush-type varieties could work. Position the pots well and water more often than you would if the plants were in open ground.

Always use well-drained containers or pots.

Eating beans

Prepare green beans by topping and tailing to remove stalks. Runner beans should be topped, tailed and sliced before cooking. Small green beans can often be left whole or cut into two or three pieces. Always use beans that are not stringy, where possible. If runner beans have grown quite large, they may be a little stringy, but when removing the top of the bean you should be able to pull the strings from the sides with ease.

Beans should always be cooked thoroughly before eating as they contain a poison in their raw state. Cooking neutralises the problem and they can be safely eaten once cooked.

Beans can be cooled and eaten cold after cooking, and added to any cold dish. French or runner beans are particularly good to mix into a green salad. The larger beans such as butter beans and flageolet beans are also excellent salad ingredients.

Green Bean Salad

Always cook beans before eating, even if they are fresh and organic.

Ingredients:
1 lb (450 g) small green beans
4 oz (100 g) feta cheese, crumbled or cut into small pieces
1 small lettuce
A handful of baby spinach leaves
A handful of watercress, roughly chopped
1–2 tablespoons of black olives, pitted
1 tablespoon of finely chopped chives
Vinaigrette dressing

Method:
1. Steam or boil beans until tender, drain well and leave to cool.
2. Arrange lettuce leaves, spinach and watercress in a serving dish.
3. When beans are completely cold, spoon on to the bed of leaves with the olives and feta cheese.
4. Sprinkle over the chopped chives to garnish and leave in a cool place.
5. Pour over the vinaigrette dressing just before serving.

GARLIC BEANS
Cook the beans until tender and drain. In a wok or large frying pan heat a little oil and cook a couple of chopped garlic cloves for a minute or two. Add the beans and some chopped basil and stir gently until thoroughly re-heated. Serve hot.

BLACK PEPPERED BEANS
Runner beans are perfect for this dish although any green beans will do. Cook beans until tender and drain well. Toss in a little melted butter and freshly ground black pepper. Serve immediately.

Beans and Bacon

This recipe will really encourage the kids to eat their green vegetables!

Ingredients:
1 ½ lbs (700 g) green beans, cut into small pieces
1 onion, chopped
3 fl oz (100 mls) vegetable, chicken or ham stock
A couple of rashers of cooked bacon, chopped
1 teaspoon fresh thyme
A little butter or cooking oil

Method:
1. In a heavy-based saucepan, gently heat the butter or cooking oil and cook chopped onion until it starts to soften, stirring to prevent sticking.
2. Stir in the green beans, cooked bacon, thyme and stock. Mix well and bring to the boil.
3. Reduce heat and simmer for 10–15 minutes, or until beans are tender.
4. Serve hot with any dish.

Green beans can be added to soups, stews, casseroles and curry dishes, as well as being a perfect vegetable to serve with your favourite Sunday roast.

HOUSEHOLD TIPS

- Use dried beans to bake your pastry cases 'blind'. Pour beans over a sheet of greaseproof paper covering your pastry case and the pastry will set but not rise.
- Try making bean bags. Sew two squares of strong cloth together and fill with beans before sewing the last seam. Small bean bags make great toys for the kids and larger ones can be used as cushions or comfy footstools.
- Beans can also be used in place of missing counters for board games.

BROCCOLI

About broccoli

Broccoli is a member of the brassica family and, although many varieties of brassica have been consumed since ancient times, broccoli wasn't cultivated until the sixteenth century. It started off as a garden vegetable in Italy but took a few hundred years until it reached all corners of Europe and America. In the UK before the turn of the twentieth century broccoli was considered to be a strange food, but around the beginning of the twentieth century it was finally cultivated commercially and became an everyday vegetable. It is now regarded as one of the super-foods.

There are different varieties of broccoli but generally they will all grow well in a moderate climate, and are a useful and practical addition to the vegetable garden.

Properties of broccoli

Broccoli has become known as a super-food in recent years with good reason. It's packed with vitamins and minerals and is considered to be a powerful anti-oxidant, eliminating free radicals and boosting the immune system.

It has significant quantities of vitamin B5 (pantothenic acid) as well as dietary fibre, and is a vegetable worthy of everyday use. With regard to vitamins and minerals, broccoli doesn't differ that much from the other members of the brassica family such as cabbage and kale, although it is easy to grow and very practical to cook with as it needs little preparation. It can also be tastier than other brassicas.

Purple-sprouting broccoli is higher in antioxidants and an attractive alternative to regular varieties.

Growing broccoli

Brassicas, including all broccoli varieties, won't thrive in an acidic soil. If your soil has a high level of acid, incorporate lime into the soil before planting. It's also a good idea to dig in plenty of well-rotted manure or organic fertiliser during the autumn or winter before sowing seed.

Broccoli prefers a sunny position but will tolerate part shade. Choose a spot out of wind tunnels or frost pockets as plants will keep growing late in the year. Dig over the ground and remove any perennial weeds and non-organic debris. Although broccoli is a fairly hardy plant, it likes a good clean soil to thrive and crop well. The area must also be well drained.

Broccoli seed generally needs to be kept warm during the germination period and therefore they are best started off in a greenhouse or conservatory or other warm place indoors. Check on the manufacturer's sowing recommendations on your seed packet, but usually broccoli seed is sown in early spring.

Fill well-drained seed trays with fresh compost and sow seed fairly thinly. Label the trays, especially if you are growing other brassica plants, as they all look very similar in the early stages of growth and can be difficult to tell apart. Keep warm and watered until plants have three or four true leaves, not counting the first two.

Broccoli seed can be sown outside in a seedbed a little later in the year but may need protecting with a cloche or similar covering overnight.

When your seedlings are ready to plant out, water the compost well before removing them from the trays. Handle as little as possible and try not to touch the roots too much as any root damage could affect the growth of the plant. Plant out in a prepared bed allowing about 18–24 in (45–60 cm) between plants and around 2 ft (60 cm) between rows. Double-check on your seed packet for variations.

Weed regularly and water often, especially in dry periods. Watch out for cabbage white butterfly attacks. It's always nice to see butterflies in the garden but the cabbage white butterfly will lay its eggs on the underside of brassica leaves, and when the caterpillars hatch out they can devour whole plants before you even notice they are there.

If you see cabbage white butterflies hovering around your broccoli patch, the following morning check on the underside of the leaves and destroy any eggs that are laid there. Remove the leaf if necessary or scrape the eggs off gently – but do get rid of them. Planting strong smelling herbs close by will sometimes deter the butterfly but don't rely on it.

When plants start producing the flower heads, cut with a sharp knife and eat them. Don't wait for the heads to get large as they may turn to flowers very quickly. Generally for the home grower, removing the first stalk will encourage others to follow. This will mean many small broccoli heads rather than one large one. The plants will keep producing for longer and the smaller the stalks the tastier they are.

Cut broccoli as often as you can. If you have too much to eat, it will keep for a couple of days in the fridge or break into small florets and freeze quickly on trays. Broccoli will keep for many months in a freezer. Remember to label the container or freezer bag before storing.

As long as containers are fairly large, well-drained and regularly watered, there's no reason why broccoli shouldn't be grown in containers or pots. Broccoli likes a sunny spot so they should be positioned well.

There are dwarf varieties of broccoli available in seed form from good garden suppliers. These varieties may be more suitable if large containers aren't available.

Eating broccoli

Broccoli can be eaten raw although most people find the taste rather too strong. A few very tiny florets broken off a larger head of broccoli can be mixed into a salad bowl. This results in a nutty flavour and makes an interesting addition to a regular green salad, without being overpowering in taste.

Generally, though, broccoli is cooked but shouldn't be overcooked. Steam or boil until just tender.

Cooking with broccoli

Broccoli and Cheese

Another recipe to encourage the kids to eat their green vegetables! Cauliflower can be used instead of broccoli if preferred.

Ingredients:
Broccoli florets, to serve 2–4 people

For the sauce:
2 oz (50 g) butter
2 oz (50 g) flour
2 oz (50 g) finely grated hard cheese
½ pint (300 mls) milk
Seasoning

Method:

1. Steam or boil broccoli until just cooked. Drain well and put into an ovenproof dish.
2. Make the sauce while the broccoli is cooking:
3. Melt butter in a pan over a low heat then stir in the flour and stir over a low heat for a few minutes.
4. Remove from the heat and gradually add the milk stirring all the time to prevent lumps forming.
5. Return to the heat and bring to the boil, then reduce heat and simmer for 2–3 minutes until sauce thickens, stirring all the time.
6. Remove from the heat, season and quickly stir in the grated cheese. Keep stirring until cheese has melted.
7. Pour sauce over the broccoli and grill under a medium heat for a few minutes until golden brown.
8. Dish could also be popped into a warm oven for 10 minutes instead of grilling if preferred.

Broccoli and Fennel Soup

Fennel adds a taste of *je ne sais quoi* to this broccoli soup.

Ingredients:
3 broccoli heads
1 fennel bulb, chopped into fairly small pieces
2–3 tablespoons chopped sage
About 2 pints (1.1 litres) chicken or vegetable stock

Method:

1. Bring stock to the boil in a large pan and add fennel pieces.
2. Reduce heat and simmer for 5–10 minutes.
3. Separate broccoli florets and slice the stems thinly.
4. Add all broccoli and sage to the pan and stir.
5. Bring back to the boil, adding more stock if required.
6. Reduce heat and simmer for 10–15 minutes until all vegetables are tender.
7. Remove from the heat and allow to cool slightly.
8. Blend in a liquidiser or food processor until smooth.
9. Return to the pan and re-heat very gently, stirring all the time, for a few minutes until hot right through.
10. Serve hot with crusty bread or croutons.

Broccoli Quiche

Broccoli turns an everyday quiche into a taste sensation.

Ingredients:

A handful of broccoli florets
2 eggs, beaten
5 fl oz (150 mls) milk or single cream
4 oz (100 g) grated hard cheese
Seasoning
6 oz short-crust pastry:
To make your own pastry case, follow instructions under tomato quiche on page 8.

Method:

1. Pre-heat oven to gas mark 6 (400°F, 200°C).
2. Make pastry case and bake blind as for tomato quiche. Leave the oven on. Remove beans and greaseproof paper.
3. Boil or steam broccoli florets and drain well.

4. Lay broccoli on pastry and cover with grated cheese.
5. Beat eggs and milk or cream together and season.
6. Pour over the broccoli and cheese.
7. Bake in pre-heated oven for about 30 minutes until golden brown.
8. Serve hot or cold. Perfect with a green salad.

ASPARAGUS

About asparagus

Asparagus is often considered to be a luxury food, probably because of the price we pay for it in the shops. Asparagus is in fact a very practical crop to grow in the home vegetable garden. It is available before most other summer vegetables are ready and is also a perennial crop that will keep coming back every year. With a little TLC plants will grow and provide more asparagus than you and your family could possibly eat!

Asparagus is indigenous to coastal areas and thrives with seaweed fertilisers and dressings. It was documented by the Romans, who prized it as a medicinal as well as a culinary vegetable. There are records of asparagus being cultivated in ancient Egyptian times, although it didn't become a popular vegetable in Europe and America until the sixteenth century.

Properties of asparagus

Asparagus is a nutritious vegetable and is said to have many medicinal qualities. High in vitamins and minerals, it is a worthy vegetable to add to your everyday diet. It is low in calories and is also believed to help alleviate symptoms of kidney disorders. It can be safely eaten raw as well as cooked.

Asparagus helps cancel water retention in the body and the water in which asparagus is cooked makes a healthy and nutritious drink.

Asparagus is one of the few garden vegetables with a significant quantity of vitamin E, which is more often found in nuts and seeds.

Growing asparagus

One thing that puts a lot of people off growing asparagus is that you have to wait for three years or more before the spears can be used if you grow from seed, and a full crop won't be available for five years. However, asparagus 'crowns' can be bought in garden centres and will be ready to use in the year after planting, if you buy three-year-old crowns.

If you decide to start your asparagus from seed, it is definitely more satisfying but you will have to look after the plants until they are ready to be harvested. Read through the manufacturer's growing recommendations on the seed packet for exact instructions for your variety and region.

Three-year-old crowns should be bought from a reputable supplier and, if they come with any special instructions, read before planting. Male crowns are better if you can find them. Female crowns put energy into developing seed so won't produce as many spears as male plants.

Asparagus is a perennial and a healthy plant will last many years. A permanent patch should be given over to them as they are better left in one place rather than disturbed. Because they will stay in the same place for the foreseeable future, the more you prepare before planting, the better.

The soil should have a pH of 6.5 to 7.5 and it is worth testing your soil before planting the crowns. Once you have all the elements in order, asparagus plants will crop for 15 years or more, so it's well worth getting the balance right to begin with.

Asparagus thrives in full sun so a sunny position should be chosen, although the plants will get fairly tall after they have finished cropping each year so care should be taken that they don't over shadow other plants. A raised bed system on the northern side of your garden is ideal if possible. It must be a well-drained spot.

Dig over the ground as deeply as you can and remove any perennial weeds, non-organic debris and large stones. Incorporate sand or any other products you need to get the pH balance right and add as much fertiliser as you can. Asparagus is native to coastal areas and thrives in a soil rich with seaweed and sand additives.

During the spring or whenever the crowns are available, plant about 6 in (15 cm) deep and allow 12–18 in (30–45 cm) between plants. Cover crowns with a mixture of soil and sand. Water well but don't compact the soil. After a couple of weeks, asparagus will start showing through, but should not be cut in the first year. Keep free of weeds and watered during hot dry weather and allow the plants to produce ferns and die back on their own.

Early in the following spring, cut down the ferns. Wear gloves when you do this as they can be sharp. In subsequent years, ferns should be cut down in the autumn and a layer of seaweed spread over the whole area. Any un-rotted material should be removed in the spring. Then add sand and soil to increase the height of the bed. Asparagus crowns will grow bigger every year and the bed will need raising to accommodate them.

During the second year, harvest the spears when they are around 6 in (15 cm) or so, by cutting with a sharp knife as close to the surface of the soil as possible. Cut early in the morning and rinse under very cold water to prevent the spears from becoming limp. Keep harvesting until around mid-June or when the plants start producing ferns.

In late summer or early autumn, asparagus beetle can attack. Watch out for them and pick them off or treat with an organic product to get rid of them. They won't kill the plant, but the crop may be affected the following year. Cutting back the ferns will help deter the beetle.

To produce your own asparagus seed, leave the ferns to grow if you have female plants and allow them to develop seed. Collect the seed when fully ripe and sow in well-drained trays of compost until they have germinated. Transplant them into pots and look after them for a couple of years before putting out into the garden. Don't cut the spears in the first three or four years though as this will weaken the plants.

Although this all sounds rather involved and time consuming, once the plants have become established, very little maintenance is required and the asparagus spears you harvest year after year will be well worth the effort.

It's unusual to grow asparagus in containers as they tend to get larger every year and don't particularly like to be moved. However, if the conditions are very close to open-ground conditions, it may be worth trying a plant or two.

Make sure the pots or containers are large enough to allow for growth and have a good mix of soil and seaweed type products. They must be well-drained and in a sunny, airy spot, and of course they should be watered regularly.

Eating asparagus

Asparagus comes early in the year when other vegetables are just getting started in the garden, so they are always a welcome addition to the dinner table, and can be eaten cooked or raw.

ASPARAGUS SALADS

A few young spears of raw asparagus cut in half are a nutritious and tasty addition to the salad bowl. Or make an asparagus side salad. Cut a few fresh asparagus spears into short lengths and mix with some chopped nuts and a light dressing of nut oil. Chill for 20 or 30 minutes before serving.

Cooking with asparagus

Asparagus can be lightly boiled or steamed to accompany almost any meal. When just cooked, drain well and toss in a little butter. Avoid over-cooking. Experiment with adding a few chopped fresh herbs or black pepper if liked. Stir in after cooking.

Asparagus Omelette

Make an omelette fit for royalty at any time of the day.

Ingredients:

Eggs (allow 2 per person for a main meal, or 1 per person for a snack)
Asparagus spears (2–4 per omelette)
Crumbled feta cheese or grated hard cheese
Sunflower oil
Seasoning
A little cooking oil

Method:

1. Cut half the asparagus spears into short lengths. Leave the others whole then steam or boil all asparagus gently for a few minutes until just cooked. Drain well and keep warm.
2. Beat eggs well and stir in the cheese and seasoning.
3. Heat oil in a frying pan and pour in the egg mixture.
4. Add the cut pieces of asparagus and cook gently over a fairly low heat for a few minutes.

5. Turn the omelette over and cook the other side gently for a further few minutes or until the egg is set.
6. Fold omelette in half and place a couple of uncut asparagus spears on top.
7. Serve hot.

Asparagus Soup

In the early summer months, this wonderful vegetable will fill the gap between winter and late summer crops.

Ingredients:

1 lb (450 g) asparagus, cut into small pieces
1 or 2 medium-sized onions, thinly sliced
2 pints (1.1 litres) vegetable or chicken stock
3 oz (75 g) butter (or low fat alternative)
Seasoning

Method:

1. Melt the butter over a low heat in a large pan.
2. Add prepared asparagus and onion and stir gently for a few minutes until vegetables start to soften.
3. Add the stock to the pan and bring to the boil.
4. Reduce the heat and simmer for about 40 minutes until vegetables are cooked through.
5. Season with a little salt and pepper (or a handful of fresh chopped herbs if preferred) and serve immediately.

For a smooth creamy soup, blend in a liquidiser or food processor and re-heat gently for a few minutes. Swirl a little cream in bowls just before serving.

COURGETTES

About courgettes

Courgettes (or zucchini) didn't become a popular vegetable in Europe and America until the early twentieth century, although marrows had been grown for many years before that. Although marrows are nutritious and a useful kitchen garden vegetable to grow, they are nowhere near as tasty as young courgettes.

Courgettes are part of the very large squash family, which also includes pumpkins, cucumbers, and so on. Many of the squash vegetables originated in America, but courgettes became popular in the Mediterranean area, when the Italians started eating young immature marrows. They then became a vegetable in their own right. Courgettes will grow in a moderate climate and only need a little extra protection if started off early in the year.

Properties of courgettes

Courgettes are a good source of niacin (vitamin B3) and other vitamins, including vitamin A. The seeds have a mixture of natural chemicals that have been found to help reduce enlargement of the prostate gland, which is a common condition in men aged over 50.

Courgettes are a good source of folate, potassium and manganese and are very low in calories. Plants can produce an overwhelming number of fruits, and are often given away during the growing season. Courgette flowers are also a nutritious delicacy. The flowers are short-lived and not easy to transport, making them an expensive food to buy.

Growing courgettes

Courgettes are probably one of the easiest vegetables to grow. There are a number of interesting varieties to grow in the home vegetable garden. The regular courgette resembles a cucumber but there are different shapes and colours available from most garden suppliers.

Courgette plants are very similar to most squash plants in the early stages of development and, if you are growing pumpkins and cucumbers as well as courgettes, remember to label the seed trays or pots, as it's almost impossible to tell the difference between seedlings.

Choose a sunny well-drained spot in the garden. Courgettes will tolerate partial shade, but double-check on the manufacturer's growing recommendations on your seed packet for variations. Some growers like to plant squash plants on a ridge or mound. Courgettes often come up on their own in a compost heap.

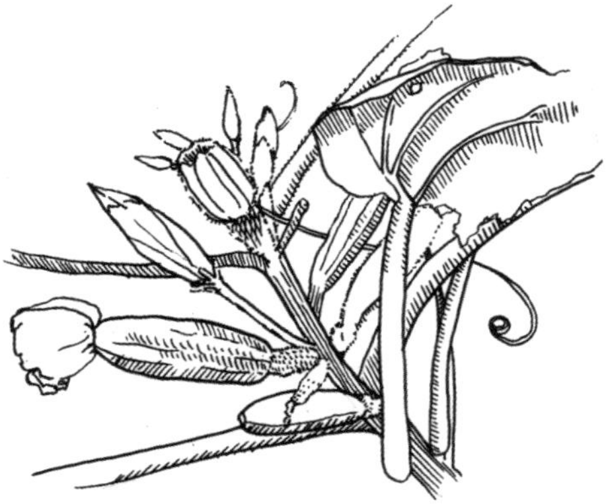

Dig over the ground and remove any perennial weeds and non-organic debris. Rake over to a fairly fine consistency.

Start courgette seed off in the spring in a greenhouse, conservatory or indoors in a bright spot. Prepare well-drained pots with fresh compost and sow two seeds per pot. If both seeds germinate, remove the weaker one and leave the other to grow on. Biodegradable pots can be used to avoid damaging roots when transplanting, although courgettes are fairly hardy and, as long as the roots aren't over-handled, they should transplant without harm.

Keep your pots watered, but never waterlogged, and in a warm place until all danger of frost has passed and the plants have at least three or four true leaves. Because courgettes grow rapidly, it's worth sowing just a few early in the year and then sowing seed directly outside a little later.

Transplant courgettes to your prepared bed in the morning of a warm sunny day, ideally. Soak the pots with water before removing the plants. Tip the whole contents of the pot out gently and try not to handle the roots too much.

Plant out allowing 18–24 in (45–60 cm) per plant. This seems like a huge space for such small plants but they will grow into it very quickly. Water well after planting and keep weeds away in the early stages of growth. Make sure the plants never dry out and watch out for slug or snail attacks. They can wipe out all your plants in no time, if they get a chance. Use any organic method of slug repellent that you can. Crushed egg shells and sand work well, but will need replacing often, or try old fashioned remedies such as a bowl of beer. Whatever you do, protect your plants from slugs and snails.

In a very short time courgette plants will grow, and slugs and snails will move on to younger plants. The foliage shades the soil around each plant deterring weeds, so once they have become established all you really need to do is make sure they don't dry out.

As soon as the plants start producing courgettes, start using them. Don't wait until they get too big. The plants will crop more and more so you are better off using them while they are small and tastier. Cut through the stalk using a sharp knife, being careful not to damage the plant.

Courgettes are large, fast growing plants and will come up of their own accord in random places around the garden. Growing in containers is a little trickier though.

Use large well-drained containers with rich, fresh compost, and water more than usual. Courgettes have a high water content and therefore need lots of water to thrive. Never let pots become waterlogged though.

Eating courgettes

There are many ways to enjoy courgettes and, if you are growing your own, you'll probably find yourself with so many you will need to get creative in the kitchen.

STIR-FRIES

Cut courgettes into fairly thin slices and add to the other vegetables in the pan. If the peel is a little tough, cook for slightly longer. Young courgettes need very little cooking, just a minute or two in a stir-fry.

ONE-POT MEALS

Cut courgettes into small pieces and add to bolognese or chilli dishes. You can also slice courgettes and place them between layers of lasagne pasta to add bulk; this is especially good in a vegetarian lasagne.

COURGETTES AND HERBS

Courgettes can be served as a side vegetable. Steam or bring to the boil in a saucepan, reduce the heat and simmer until tender. Drain well. Return to the pan and stir in a little butter and chopped fresh herbs of your choice.

Courgette Pasta Salad

Leftover peppers or other veggies can be added to this dish.

Ingredients:

4 courgettes
2 tomatoes
3 or 4 spring onions, or 1 small red onion
1 or 2 cloves of garlic
1 tablespoon chopped parsley
Seasoning
Preferred salad dressing
6 oz (175 g) pasta shells

Method:

1. Slice the courgettes and put into a large pan. Cover with water and bring to the boil.
2. Reduce heat and simmer for about 5 minutes, until tender. Drain well and leave to cool.
3. Cook the pasta shells in boiling water then drain well.
4. Put pasta shells into serving dish and stir in a little salad dressing. Leave to cool.
5. Chop tomatoes, onions, parsley and garlic (or crush garlic if preferred).
6. When pasta and courgettes are completely cold, stir all the ingredients together. Season to taste.
7. Chill for 10–20 minutes before serving.

Ratatouille

Make enough ratatouille for two days and keep cooled leftovers in the fridge overnight.

Ingredients:

1 aubergine – if available
2 courgettes
1 or 2 sweet peppers
3 or 4 large tomatoes
1 or 2 medium onions
Seasoning
Fresh herbs, such as basil (optional)
A little cooking oil

Method:

1. If using an aubergine, cut in half and sprinkle with salt. Leave for 30 minutes then rinse off the salt and cut into slices.
2. Slice courgettes and chop onions, peppers and tomatoes.
3. Heat a little oil in a wok or deep frying pan and add all the vegetables.

4. Stir over a low heat until all vegetables are tender. Add more tomatoes or a little tomato puree and water if the mix seems a little dry.
5. Stir in chopped fresh herbs and seasoning to taste. Cook for a further minute or two and serve hot.

CHEESY COURGETTES

Slice the courgettes. Put them into a pan and cover with water. Bring to the boil, reduce heat and simmer for about 5 minutes or until cooked. Drain well and put into an ovenproof dish. Sprinkle some grated cheese on top and pop into the oven or under a medium grill for a few minutes to brown.

Alternatively, make or buy a cheese or mushroom sauce and pour over the courgettes, then brown off as above.

HOUSEHOLD TIPS

- Courgettes are a squash and as with most edible squashes, the seeds are beneficial. They are said to keep the body free from intestinal parasites so can help prevent tummy bugs, especially on holiday – although explaining the reason for the courgette seeds in your suitcase to custom officials at the airport could prove difficult!

CHAPTER 4

HERB CORNER

Herbs and spices can transform a simple mince and pasta dish into a delicious lasagne with an Italian flavour, or a simple French loaf into a mouth-watering garlic bread dripping with herbs and butter.

Herbs have been cultivated for thousands of years. Many were used in medicinal preparations, some of which we still use today. During the Middle Ages, herbalists were in danger of being burned at the stake for using what was considered to be magic at the time. Often in such cases, herbs were the perfect remedy for an illness that traditional medicines of the time had failed to treat.

This chapter covers 12 everyday herbs and spices that can be used in the kitchen and for medicinal use:

- basil
- bay
- chives

- coriander
- fennel
- garlic
- mint
- oregano
- parsley
- rosemary
- sage
- thyme.

Herbs are an attractive and practical addition to the garden. Design a herb garden or grow them along pathways or among the flowers and vegetables. The French invented *le potager* to save space in the garden, by growing herbs around small vegetable beds. Many herbs have aromatic and lush foliage and will brighten up any corner of the garden. They also help deter pests and bugs because of their strong scent.

Many herbs are perennial and will come back year after year. A herb garden needs very little maintenance once established.

Most herbs can also be grown in pots and containers, and many can be successfully grown indoors on a sunny windowsill. Herbs should be used regularly to encourage more growth, and more brownie points in the kitchen!

BASIL

About basil

Basil is commonly known as the 'tomato herb' and is an annual plant that needs to be sown every year in a moderate climate. In warmer climates plants can be biennial. Basil has been cultivated for literally thousands of years as a medicinal and culinary herb and many myths and legends are attached to it. It was believed to be the herb of love, attracting your soulmate if a sprig of basil was worn behind the ear.

On a more practical note, however, it is a good fly repellent and a pot of fresh basil near an open window or door in your house will deter flies.

Growing basil

Basil is indigenous to warm regions and won't survive cold temperatures. Start your seeds in a greenhouse, conservatory or a warm place indoors. Sow in well-drained trays or pots of fresh compost. Water regularly but don't allow the compost to become waterlogged.

After all danger of frost has past, and your seedlings are large enough to handle, they can be transplanted out into the garden. Choose a sunny spot, preferably with your tomato plants (so you don't forget to use it).

Prepare the ground before planting out by digging over, removing any perennial weeds and raking to a fine tilth. Basil plants are fairly hardy and don't grow very big so can be dotted around the garden wherever you have a space. Check on your seed packet for spacing recommendations for your variety if you are planting out in lines.

Basil likes full sun and drying out can be a problem. Make sure they get plenty of water. Keep weed-free, especially in the early stages of growth, and protect from slugs and snails. Basil isn't normally attractive to pests in the garden, and when established and growing well there shouldn't be any problems.

Basil seed can be planted directly in the garden, but a little later in the year. Check on the recommendations for your particular variety.

Use leaves as soon as the plant is growing well. Pinch out flower heads when they arrive to encourage more leaves. Fresh leaves will store for a few days in the fridge, or they can be dried for use in the winter. Hang sprigs upside down in a dark airy room until very dry. Crumble into clean glass jars. Label and store out of direct light.

Basil can be successfully grown in pots and containers and is an excellent 'windowsill' herb. Always use fresh compost in well-drained pots and water regularly. Basil likes a sunny spot but leaves may be scorched if they are positioned behind glass in strong sunlight. Shade during the hottest part of the day if necessary.

There are a number of different varieties of basil seed available. They are attractive indoor pot plants as well as outdoors on a patio or scattered around the garden.

Eating basil

Basil is the perfect herb to enhance the taste of tomatoes and will bring the taste of many everyday dishes alive.

- Chop fresh basil leaves finely and sprinkle on pizza before cooking.
- Use a small sprig of basil to garnish any meal.
- Add finely chopped leaves to sauces for pasta dishes or bolognese.

Basil is an excellent herb to add to wine vinegar or oil. Simply add a sprig or two to a bottle of white wine vinegar and leave for a few days to steep before using. Or add to olive oil. Seal the bottle after adding basil and keep in a warm cupboard for a few weeks.

HOUSEHOLD TIPS

- A pot of fresh basil growing near an open window or door will help repel flies during the summer months.
- Basil has mild sedative properties and will help alleviate stomach cramps. An infusion of basil leaves sipped slowly can soothe headaches and relax the body.

BAY

About bay

Bay is an important culinary herb and is the main ingredient in *bouquet garni*, a mix of herbs that no chef would be without. Bay leaves, in Roman times, were strung into crowns for the victor in physical combat. It has been used as an antiseptic herb but generally is cultivated for culinary use only.

Also known as bay laurel, it is an evergreen shrub, usually grown in containers in more moderate climates. The containers should be kept in a warm place during the winter months if possible. In warmer climates, a bay tree can grow to 15 metres tall.

Growing bay

Bay plants can be started from autumn cuttings or layering branches from an existing plant. To layer a branch, simply pull a long lower branch from a well-established plant to the ground and hold in place with a V-shaped peg. Cover with soil and leave to produce roots. Water gently. During the following year, when the new plant is growing, the original branch can be cut away and the new plant moved.

Cuttings from bay trees should be pushed into compost, cut end down, and watered. Keep in a fairly warm place until roots have developed. The plant can then be transplanted if necessary.

Choose a fairly large well-drained container in which to grow your bay tree. In cold winters it's advisable to bring the plant indoors, so you will need to be able to move it.

During the summer months, bay can often die back through lack of water. The soil in containers and pots dries out quickly and care should be taken to water bay trees regularly. Water very occasionally in the winter, and only when the soil feels dry.

Bay can also be grown from seed although germination rates can be poor. Lay seed on moist compost in a well-drained container and cover with a fine layer of dry compost. Keep in a warm dark place until seedlings appear. Look after seedlings until the plants become large enough to handle and then transplant to their final position in the garden or into their own containers.

The fruits of bay aren't edible but if left to mature they will produce seed.

As with most aromatic herbs, bay rarely suffers from pests and diseases and should thrive for many years with enough heat and water. Re-pot using fresh compost every few years. Keep your containers of bay in a sunny position in the garden or on a patio during the summer.

Unless you live in an area with very mild winters and have a large space available, bay is almost always better grown in containers. As the containers should be fairly large and will need wheeling inside in very cold temperatures, a trolley or pot mover may be a good investment.

Bay doesn't mind its roots being squashed together, so won't need re-potting every year. Make sure the container is well-drained and watered regularly. During the winter, less water is required.

Eating bay

Bay leaves are waxy in texture and are best removed at the end of the cooking time. Alternatively, they can be dried and crumbled into a dish. They have a slightly bitter taste but compliment many recipes.

- Add a few whole bay leaves to stews and casseroles. Remove before serving.
- Fresh or crumbled dried leaves can also be added to soups and most one-pot meals.
- There is no specific recipe for *bouquet garni* but you can make your own. Using a non-plastic string, tie together sprigs of thyme, parsley and a few bay leaves. Other herbs can be added according to taste, such as celery leaves, tarragon and rosemary. Add the bunch of herbs to your recipe early in the cooking time and remove before serving.

Keep a few dried leaves in a sealed jar for use when the plant is resting during the winter months. Bay tends to have just as much flavour when dried as it does fresh.

HOUSEHOLD TIPS

- Bay is a useful decorative plant during the winter and has traditionally been used in winter decorations for Christmas and other celebrations. Get the children making centrepieces for the festive dinner table. Mix with holly and other evergreens for a spectacular display.
- Noblemen wore head-dresses of bay as far back as Roman times.

CHIVES

About chives

Chives are a member of the onion group and are an easy herb to grow. They are perennial and, once established, will keep growing for many years. Chives grow wild in many parts of Europe and America and have been collected for culinary use for centuries. They originate from China.

Being part of the onion family, they aid digestion and will also help alleviate cold and flu symptoms, although onions are probably more effective as a medicinal aid.

There are a number of different types of chive seed available, including a 'garlic' tasting variety sometimes called Chinese chives. Chive plants produce purple or white flowers, which are edible and can be used as a garnish.

Growing chives

Most plants in the onion family are difficult to germinate from seed. Chives, however, are easy to get going and, once established, a clump of chives will last for many years. They sometimes die back in the winter but will return in the spring. A pot of chives on a windowsill will ensure fresh chives all year round.

Sow seed in well-drained pots or trays of fresh compost and keep watered but not over-watered until seedlings appear. When the plants are big enough to handle they can be transplanted into the garden or individual pots.

Plant out chive plants during the evening when the weather has warmed up, and choose a sunny spot in the garden. In a very hot dry period they may need a little protection from the sun. Chives make an attractive border plant, as well as a useful herb to include in the herb garden. Water the plants well during the summer.

Start using chives when the plant is growing well and looks healthy and strong. Cut with scissors from the outside of each clump, down to about two inches from the ground. Use regularly and they will thrive.

When the plant has finished flowering, chives should be cut down to a couple of inches high and, weather permitting, should start producing more leaves.

In the autumn, clumps can be divided if they are getting too big. Using a fork, dig around the plant and lift, being careful not to damage the roots. Separate the roots into two or more pieces and re-plant immediately.

Chive flowers can be eaten fresh and used as a garnish and can also be dried for winter use. The leaves won't dry well, but a few can be frozen if necessary. Freeze quickly on a tray, pack and label. Chives can normally be grown inside and outdoors all year round and storing is usually unnecessary.

Chives work well in pots and containers as long as they are growing in fresh compost, watered regularly and have enough light. They also like to be used!

Chives are a perfect windowsill herb to have in the kitchen although, as with any plants, direct sunlight through glass can scorch leaves and dry out the compost very quickly. Allow your plant a little shade from direct sunlight but always keep it in a light airy place.

Eating chives

Chives will add a mild onion flavour to all your favourite dishes. Cut into small pieces with kitchen scissors or chop finely with a sharp knife before using.

- Stir into a green salad or any mixed salad bowl.
- Make a potato salad. Steam or boil potatoes until tender. Drain well and cut into cubes, then leave to cool. Make a dressing of half mayonnaise and half natural yoghurt and add a handful of fresh chopped chives. When the potatoes are completely cold, stir in the dressing. Chill for 10 minutes before serving.
- Add chopped chives to beaten eggs before cooking an omelette or add to the pan after eggs have been cooking for a few minutes.
- Top cheese on toast with chopped chives and grill for a few seconds longer.

Chopped chives can be used as a garnish for many meals, from salads to meat and vegetable dishes.

CORIANDER

About coriander

Coriander is probably the most widely used herb round the world and is easy to grow. Fresh leaves add a distinct spicy flavour to any dish. Coriander seed is often added to sweet dishes.

Traditionally coriander was used to aid digestion and, although generally considered to be a culinary herb, it was used in many medicinal preparations throughout the centuries. Ancient Chinese cultures believed it to bestow immortality and seeds have been found in tombs over 5,000 years old.

Native to southern Europe and parts of Asia, it now grows wild in many parts of the world. It is an annual herb and should be planted every year, if the plants do not re-seed themselves.

Growing coriander

Coriander seed should be sown *in situ* as the seedlings don't transplant well. It likes a sunny spot but tends to run to seed quickly in too much sun. Grow some in partial shade and some in direct sun. The plants in the sunny spot will produce seed you can use in the kitchen or sow the following year. The plants in the semi-shady spot will produce more foliage and can be used fresh for many months.

Prepare the ground in early spring and rake to a fine tilth. Remove any perennial weeds and large stones. The seeds are large and easy to handle and should be placed about 1.5 in (4 cm) apart in shallow drills. Sow a short line every few weeks throughout spring and summer. Cover with a cloche at night if a frost is expected. When the seedlings are a few inches high, thin to allow about 8 in (20 cm) of growing room per plant. Pull out the weaker plants.

Although coriander is an annual plant, it will often re-seed itself, and a coriander patch can keep going for many years. It will probably find its way around the garden but the plants aren't intrusive like mint – if they get in the way, simply pull them up and use in the kitchen.

Coriander has a strong scent and, like most herbs, will deter aphids and other pests. Plant among your vegetable crops. It needs very little looking after once established.

Coriander leaves can be dried and stored for many months before they lose their flavour. Hang sprigs upside down in a dark airy place until dry and then crumble into jars and label. Store out of direct light.

Coriander grows well in containers. Make sure the container or pot is well-drained and not allowed to dry out.

Coriander tends to run to seed or 'bolt' in very hot sun or when there is a lack of water. Shade from direct sunlight through glass and water regularly to encourage your plants to produce more foliage than seed.

Eating coriander

Coriander is a must-have herb for food lovers. It is an essential ingredient in curries and other spicy dishes.

- To make a simple chicken curry dish, cook chopped tomatoes with a chopped onion in a pan until the onion is soft. Add cooked chicken, cut into pieces (or use a vegetarian substitute). Mix in a handful of chopped fresh coriander and cook until the chicken is piping hot right through. Serve hot with rice or potatoes.
- Add fresh chopped coriander leaves to a bread recipe with a little olive oil.
- Stir in some chopped fresh coriander before cooking homemade burgers or rissoles.
- Use a few feathery leaves as a garnish for any dish.

Experiment with coriander in the kitchen. As well as using the leaves, seed can be ground and used as a spice.

HOUSEHOLD TIPS

- Coriander has been used in many medicinal preparations over the ages and is still accepted today as being a useful aide in digestion. Use leaves and seeds in everyday dishes to relieve pain from indigestion.
- Coriander has a very strong aroma and, like other herbs, will help deter pests from your vegetable garden.

FENNEL

About fennel

Fennel can be grown for the leaves or as a vegetable crop. Fennel has been used in many medicinal preparations over the centuries and is believed to be a useful slimming aid. There seems to be hard evidence to support this as fennel does indeed aid digestion, although it also improves appetite.

Wild or home-cultivated seed is unlikely to produce a fennel bulb and hybrid seeds should be bought if you want to grow the vegetable rather than the herb. Fennel is a loner and prefers its own space in the garden.

Fennel is really a multi-purpose plant. The seed, leaves and bulbous root are all edible and very useful in the kitchen.

Growing fennel

Fennel is probably one of the easiest plants to grow in your herb garden, although cultivating the bulbous root requires a little more attention. The biggest problem you will probably face with growing fennel is its tendency to bolt in hot dry weather, and plants can also bolt when transplanted. Water well and shade from the midday sun until plants become established to avoid this.

Use biodegradable pots, if possible, to sow your seeds. This will help make the transplanting process smoother. Sow in early spring in fresh compost and keep pots warm and watered. The pots must be well drained. Plant out the seedlings in late spring to early summer. Check on your seed packet for variations.

Dig over the ground well before planting and remove any perennial weeds. Rake over the soil. Fennel isn't fond of heavy soil so add a little sharp sand if your soil is on the heavy side. Fennel inhibits the growth of dill, coriander and tomatoes and should be positioned as far away as possible from these plants.

Seed can be planted directly outside as long as there is no danger of frost. Cover with a cloche at night if the temperature drops too much.

Each plant will need about 12 in (30 cm) of growing room. Allow about 2 ft (60 cm) between rows. Thinning will be necessary if you sow your seed directly outside in lines. Remove weaker plants.

Fennel deters white fly from your vegetable or herb bed but can be susceptible to caterpillars. Fennel can be left in the ground right through the autumn but won't survive a very heavy frost.

Use the leaves fresh. They can be dried or frozen but will lose some of their taste. Seed can be stored to add to pickles and relishes or saved to plant the following spring.

Fennel will grow successfully in well-drained pots and containers, but shouldn't be allowed to dry out. As fennel can inhibit the growth of other crops, pots or container growing may be a good way of keeping them to themselves!

Eating fennel

Fennel has a very strong aniseed aroma and flavour. It is a well-known accompaniment to fish dishes.

- Fennel seeds can be used in pickles or crushed and added to soups, homemade burgers or sausages.
- Add flowers to herbal vinegars.
- Put a sprig of fresh fennel in a light oil, cover and leave for a few days before using.
- Chopped fresh fennel should be added to sauces and soups in the last minute or so of cooking time.
- Chop fresh fennel leaves and stir into a salad.
- Use the attractive feathery leaves as a garnish.

Cooking reduces the flavour so fennel should always be added to your recipe in the last minute or two of cooking unless otherwise advised in the recipe.

HOUSEHOLD TIPS

- Fennel, with its aniseed-like flavour, provides one of the best digestive aids of the everyday herbs you can grow. It has long been considered to be a valuable addition to a weight-loss diet. Although fennel stimulates the appetite, it does help to digest food more efficiently. It is also effective in alleviating cold and flu symptoms.
- Like other aromatic herbs, fennel's strong scent will deter pests from your garden.

GARLIC

About garlic

Garlic has been cultivated for literally thousands of years and has all sorts of myths and legends attached to it, including keeping away vampires and bad spirits. Wild garlic has been around even longer. The Romans believed garlic brought strength and their soldiers were encouraged to include it in their daily diet.

Garlic is considered a useful food preservative, as well as being employed in medicinal preparations. It has effective anti-bacterial qualities and can help ward off colds and flu. Part of the onion family, garlic is strong in taste and scent and is also an easy herb to grow in the kitchen garden.

Growing garlic

Garlic is grown from the cloves of a whole bulb. It's best to buy a bulb from your garden centre to start. It can be grown from shop-bought cloves, but may not crop as well as a hybrid. If you do choose to propagate from shop-bought cloves, buy an organic variety.

Cloves can be planted early in the spring. They are a hardy plant and will tolerate cold nights. Wait until the ground is workable and dig over, pulling up any perennial weeds. Rake to a fine tilth and remove any large stones. Plant garlic cloves in lines about 8 in (20 cm) apart, root end down. Leave the tip of the cloves just above the surface of the soil, but watch out for birds, as they can pull them out of the ground at this stage.

Keep weeds away and water if necessary. Because garlic is planted early in the year, it tends to get enough rainfall to grow well. Don't let garlic dry out in hot sun though.

Garlic has anti-bacterial properties that help protect it from disease and the strong odour deters pests. The only problem garlic has is that it can run to seed. If this happens, the plant will push up a flowering stem. Bend the stem down to the ground if possible. Some growers pull these plants up as they don't store well. The cloves that have already developed can be used in the kitchen. These 'green' cloves will be stronger tasting.

Bulbs mature to full size anytime from July to September and should be harvested on a sunny day. Loosen the soil carefully around each one and pull up. Leave the plants lying on dry ground outside in the sun for a day. Store in single layers in boxes or plait and hang in a dark airy place for winter use.

Garlic will grow in well-drained pots and containers of fresh compost, although space must be allowed for full development of the bulb. Trough-like containers work well. Make sure they get plenty of light and water but avoid water logging. Garlic won't survive in stagnant water.

Plant individual cloves about 8 in (20 cm) apart. Once they are growing they shouldn't be transplanted.

Eating garlic

No good chef would be without garlic in the kitchen and a plait of garlic will encourage everyone to experiment with delicious recipes.

- Add garlic to potato recipes. See garlic potatoes in chapter two.
- Chop or crush garlic cloves and add to bolognese and chilli dishes, as well as a little in the salad bowl to bring the tastes alive.

Garlic Bread

Even the kids love garlic bread! Parsley doesn't have to be included but it does help to freshen the breath after eating strong tasting foods, such as garlic.

Ingredients:
1 large French loaf
6 oz (175 g) butter, or alternative
3–4 rncloves garlic, crushed
1 tablespoon finely chopped fresh parsley

Method:
1. Pre-heat oven to gas mark 4 (350°F, 180°C).
2. Cut slits in the French loaf, leaving about half an inch at the bottom of each cut to hold the loaf together.
3. Blend crushed garlic and parsley with butter and mix well.
4. Spread the butter mixture on every cut surface of the bread and push back together to re-form the loaf.
5. Wrap loosely in foil and bake in the centre of the oven for 15–20 minutes or until hot right through.

Every main meal recipe can be enhanced with a hint of garlic. Serve with fresh parsley to help freshen the breath.

HOUSEHOLD TIPS

- Garlic really has stood the test of time as a healing herb and has been cultivated for medicinal and culinary use for thousands of years. Garlic has strong antibiotic properties which makes it an excellent cleansing food. It also has significant amounts of dietary fibre and vitamins.
- And of course, if you hang some garlic above your front door, you will never be troubled by vampires again!

MINT

About mint

Mint is a hardy perennial and will take over the garden if left to its own devices. Mint is probably one of the most well-known herbs in the UK, if only for its perfect accompaniment to roast lamb.

It is a known digestive aid and many people swear by mint tea after a meal. There are many different varieties, including spearmint, peppermint and penny royal. In recent years there have been a number of hybrids available, such as pineapple mint and, a very recent addition, chocolate mint that really does smell like chocolate mints!

Peppermint is probably the most practical variety to grow in the herb garden as it can be used in both sweet and savoury dishes.

Growing mint

Ideally mint should be contained as it can be a very invasive herb in the garden, and will take over a whole area in no time. Use large containers where possible or sink an old bottomless bucket into the ground, fill with soil and plant mint in that. The roots will eventually find their way out, but this method of growing does help to contain the plant a little.

Mint likes moisture, although it won't live in waterlogged soil. In full sun the soil will dry out too quickly for your plants, so this is an excellent herb to grow in a shady patch in the garden where other plants may not survive.

Propagate from seed or root division. Mint germinates well and is easy to grow from seed. Sow in well-drained trays of compost and transplant when the plants are large enough to handle, either into the garden or individual pots or containers. Water regularly.

To propagate from root division, simply break off a piece of the root of an established plant. Plant in compost and keep watered and weed free until the new plant starts growing and can be transplanted, if necessary.

Mint is a hardy plant and doesn't need much looking after once established, but it shouldn't be allowed to dry out. If your plants are in a sunny spot or there has been an unusually low rainfall, a mulch can help keep moisture in the roots.

Occasionally mint suffers from a 'rust' disease. The mint rust fungus enters the plant from the soil and permanently affects the whole plant. Signs are discolouration and often a kind of 'rash' on the underside of the leaves. Plants should be removed if this occurs and new plants grown in a different area. Burn affected plants if possible to avoid spreading the disease.

Use leaves as soon as the plants start to grow, and pick off flowers to encourage more foliage. Mint can be dried successfully. Hang sprigs upside down in a dry dark airy place and crumble into jars and label. Store out of direct light.

As mint can be a very invasive herb in the garden, it's often best to grow in containers and pots. As mentioned above, sinking a bottomless bucket in the ground is a good way to grow mint in containers and it can also be grown in a shady part of the garden.

Growing mint in pots indoors can be successful but plants could struggle in direct sunlight. Allow them some shade during the day and make sure they are regularly watered.

Eating mint

Mint is a versatile herb and can be used as a digestive aid as well as a flavouring for many dishes. Peppermint and spearmint are the two most common varieties of mint used in the kitchen although there are many different types to try.

- Add fresh mint leaves in the last couple of minutes of cooking fresh peas, broad beans or new potatoes.
- Make a quick mint sauce by mixing finely chopped mint with vinegar. Leave to marinate for an hour before serving. Serve with roast lamb or any vegetable dish.
- Make tea! Pour boiling water on a sprig of mint in a jug and cover for five minutes. Stir and strain into a cup or glass.
- Experiment with mint in sweet dishes such as chocolate puddings or homemade ice cream.

HOUSEHOLD TIPS

- Mint is another ancient healing herb and, as well as being a must-have with roast lamb, it is an exceptional digestive aid. A cup of mint tea every day will soothe many digestive problems, including stomach cramps, irritable bowel syndrome and other general disorders.
- Mint tea can also relieve tension headaches without having to resort to painkillers.

OREGANO

About oregano

Oregano is sometimes known as wild marjoram. They belong to the same family but are in fact different herbs. Oregano grows wild in many parts of Europe and is a commercially viable product.

Oregano is a low-growing shrub that stays green all year round in mild climates. It is also a nutritious herb full of vitamins and minerals and worthy of a place in your herb garden. It has been used in medicinal preparations for centuries and has antiseptic and sedative qualities. Oregano is an invaluable culinary herb, and can be grown in containers and pots as well as in open ground.

Growing oregano

Oregano is a perennial herb and will come back every year, although plants are best replaced every three or four years as they can become straggly and 'woody'. Seeds germinate well and should be started quite early in the year. Put two or three seeds on to the surface of fresh compost in individual well-drained pots. Spray with water at least once or twice a day and keep in a warm place until the seedlings come up.

When the seedlings are large enough to handle, thin them to allow one seedling per pot. Plant out later when all danger of frost has passed.

Seeds can also be sown directly outside in late spring. Protect with a cloche at night until they are established and growing well. Thin plants to allow 12 in (30 cm) or more per plant, or transplant when they are large enough to handle.

The foliage is very brightly coloured, making oregano an attractive plant in the herb garden. Grow around your vegetables or as a border plant. It produces a warm humid atmosphere and is ideal to grow around a bed of sweet peppers.

Oregano is perfect for deterring aphids and plants can be placed around the vegetable garden to help keep your crops pest free.

Plants can be trimmed back and shaped, and should be used as much as possible. Start picking leaves when the plant is about 8 in (20 cm) tall. When flowers start to appear, pick off the flower heads to encourage the plant to produce more foliage.

Oregano is available fresh most of the year but can be dried for storing if needed. Hang sprigs upside down in a dark airy place. When completely dry, crumble into jars and label. Store out of direct light.

Oregano likes a sunny position and will be happy to grow in well-drained containers or hanging baskets as long as the compost doesn't dry out. Oregano is an ideal herb to grow on a patio or balcony.

Eating oregano

Oregano is useful in many everyday dishes to add that extra zest to meat and vegetables. Here are a few ideas:

- Make a chopped green mixed salad. Add crumbled feta cheese and some chopped fresh oregano. Stir gently to mix and chill for 20 minutes before serving.
- Add fresh oregano to all tomato-based dishes such as bolognese.
- Oregano can be added to stir-fries and pasta dishes.
- Place a couple of sprigs of oregano over a chicken in the last 30 minutes or so of roasting.

Oregano is an attractive herb and is a perfect garnish for all meat or vegetable dishes.

HOUSEHOLD TIPS

- Oregano has been used for centuries as a food preserver. The anti-microbe compounds in oregano help destroy microbes that may be in meats or other foods.
- Oregano aids digestion and is often used today in medicinal preparations to cure many minor ailments. A cup of oregano tea every day is packed with vitamins and minerals and will help ward off colds and flu symptoms.

PARSLEY

About parsley

Parsely is another well-known herb, but often underused. Parsley has nearly always been used as a garnish rather than added to dishes during cooking. It is however a very nutritious herb, containing significant amounts of iron and other minerals, as well as vitamins. Gram for gram, parsley has more vitamin C than citrus fruits.

There are a number of different varieties that can be used in the kitchen, including an Italian flat-leaved variety as well as the traditional curly leaf types.

Parsley is very effective in freshening the breath and should always be added to meals containing garlic. It is a biennial plant, producing flowers and seed during the second year of growth before dying back.

Growing parsley

Parsley needs to be sown every year to ensure a fresh supply of leaves. During the second year of growth the plant puts its energy into producing flowers and seeds, so there won't be much foliage available for use.

Parsley likes rich soil and a sunny spot to thrive. It will grow readily from seed but could take up to six weeks to germinate. Some growers soak seed in water before sowing to speed up the germination process.

Sow a few seeds in well-drained pots of fresh compost in the spring and keep warm and watered. When plants come up, remove the weaker ones to leave one plant per pot to grow on.

Seeds can be sown outside, but a little later in the year when all danger of frost has passed. Sow sparsely as plants will need thinning out to allow space to grow. Transplant parsley plants to a sunny spot in the garden. They will tolerate some shade but make sure the soil is rich to make up for the lack of sun. Parsley is a nutritious plant and draws its qualities from the soil. It will need an organic feed from time to time if your soil is of poor quality.

Start using leaves when the plants are about 8 in (20 cm) tall and keep using them right through the first year of growth. During the second year, allow the plants to produce flowers and seed. The seed can be collected and used in the kitchen or for sowing the following spring.

Whole stems of parsley can be frozen or dried. Lay sprigs on freezer trays and freeze quickly. Pack and label before storing. Hang sprigs up to dry in a dark airy place. Crumble into jars and label. Store out of direct light.

Parsley can be grown successfully in pots or containers on a windowsill. Choose different varieties and add some to everyday meals. Parsley is a highly nutritious food and draws many nutrients from the soil. It's therefore a good idea to start your plants in fresh compost and feed them with an organic fertiliser every few weeks.

Parsley is a biennial and will produce flower and seed during its second year of growth so fresh seed should be sown every year for a constant supply.

Eating parsley

Parsley is a perfect herb for garnishing but often gets left on the side of the plate. Chop finely and sprinkle over the dish to make it more palatable.

- Steam or boil any vegetables, drain well and toss in a little butter and finely chopped fresh parsley.
- Scrub parsley root, slice and add to stews and casseroles.

Parsley Soup

Parsley is so high in nutrients, it seems a shame to leave it on the side of the plate. This recipe is nutritious and wholesome and very economical.

Ingredients:

4 oz (100 g) fresh parsley, chopped
2 stalks of celery, finely sliced
1 onion, chopped
1 ½ pints (850 mls) vegetable or chicken stock
1 oz (25 g) butter, or alternative
1 tablespoon flour
Seasoning

Method:

1. Melt butter over a low heat in a large pan and gently cook the sliced celery and chopped onion. Stir to prevent sticking.

2. When vegetables have started to soften, stir in the flour and slowly add the stock over a low heat. Stir well.
3. Add chopped parsley and seasoning and increase heat. Bring to the boil then reduce heat and simmer for about 20 minutes.
4. Remove from heat and allow to cool. Blend in a food processor or liquidiser until smooth.
5. Return to the pan. Re-heat over a low heat stirring all the time until hot right through.
6. Serve with warm crusty bread or garlic croutons.

Parsley should be used as much as possible in the kitchen, not only for its taste but also for its wonderful nutritional qualities.

Always add parsley to garlic dishes to help freshen the breath.

ROSEMARY

About rosemary

Rosemary has many myths and legends attached to it. At various times throughout history it has been used to ward off evil spirits, and used in ceremonies such as weddings and baptisms. It has often been employed in medicinal preparations to soothe colds, headaches and digestive problems.

Rosemary is a hardy perennial and, once established in the herb garden, can last for 20 years before it needs to be replaced. It has been cultivated in herb gardens for many centuries.

More often used in cooking these days than as a medicinal herb, rosemary is invaluable in the kitchen.

Growing rosemary

Rosemary is notoriously difficult to propagate from seed. Germination is poor and can take up to three months. It is possible though, and seed should be sown in well-drained trays of fresh compost in the spring and kept warm until seedlings are ready to plant out. Check on the seed packets for manufacturer's growing recommendations before you start.

The most effective way to start off rosemary is by taking a cutting from an established plant. Although you will probably only need one or two rosemary plants in the herb garden, start off a number of cuttings in case some don't work.

Take 3–4 in (8–10 cm) cuttings just above or below a leaf joint from a healthy plant. Use a sharp knife or secateurs to avoid damage to the stem. Push cuttings, cut end down, into well-drained pots of fresh compost then water. Keep plants warm and don't allow the compost to dry out.

Cuttings should produce roots in three or four months, when they will be ready to transplant into the garden.

When you plant them in the garden, choose a well-drained sunny spot and allow 2 or 3 ft (60–90 cm) all round for the plant to grow. Water well after planting.

Rosemary is a hardy plant and will tolerate very cold weather, and often stay fresh and usable right through the winter months. The plant has also been known to survive near drought conditions, although watering fairly regularly in hot dry periods will ensure it grows well.

Although rosemary is evergreen and should be available all year round, it can be dried and stored by hanging sprigs until dry and stripping leaves off into a jar. Store out of direct light.

Rosemary is suitable for container growing although shrubs can grow quite big so plants may need re-potting every year or so.

Make sure pots are deep enough and well-drained.

Eating rosemary

Rosemary is traditionally cooked with pork, fish and chicken although it is also often eaten with roast lamb or lamb chops.

- Rosemary isn't often used in salads, but can be added to salad dressings, oils and vinegars. Place a sprig in a bottle of white wine vinegar or a light cooking oil. Seal and leave for a couple of weeks before using.
- Throw a few fresh sprigs on the coals of a barbecue. Also, leaves can be stripped and the stalks used as skewers.
- Chop leaves finely or crumble dried rosemary leaves on to pizzas, in pasta dishes and tomato sauces.

Rosemary imparts a wonderful pine aroma when burned or bruised and has a very distinctive taste.

HOUSEHOLD TIPS

- Rosemary can be used as skewers. Strip off the leaves before threading pieces of meat, fish or vegetables. The rosemary oil in the 'twig' will flavour the food as it's being cooked.
- Put a sprig or two of rosemary on the barbecue coals to help ward off mosquitoes and other night bugs.

SAGE

About sage

Sage is a hardy perennial but should be replaced every four or five years before it gets too woody. Ancient people believed it to be a herb of wisdom, hence the common name. It was grown to help drown bad smells in medieval times and the Romans believed it to be a herb of immortality.

It has been used in many medicinal preparations to treat fevers, stomach problems and even memory loss. In recent years research has proven sage to be helpful in alleviating menopausal symptoms such as hot flushes.

It has been cultivated as a medicinal and culinary herb for thousands of years. Originating in Mediterranean areas, sage is now widely grown and many varieties are available including attractive variegated types.

Growing sage

A lot of patience is needed if you want to grow sage from seed as it will be over a year before it can be used. Small plants can be bought from garden centres and larger supermarkets. Otherwise, get your sage plants going by using cuttings or by the layering method. There are many attractive varieties available, and they can be used as border plants for the herb or vegetable garden.

Sage is a woody plant and will develop roots from the stems quite readily. From a well-established plant, gently pull a healthy bottom branch down to the ground and hold in place with a V-shaped peg. Water and keep free of weeds until roots develop. Then the plant can be transplanted if necessary.

Sage can also be propagated from cuttings from a well-established plant. In the spring or summer, take 3–4 in (8–10 cm) cuttings from healthy branches and push into potting compost in well-drained containers. Keep pots warm until they start growing well, and then transplant into the garden or larger pots and containers. Sage will thrive in well-drained soil and will do well in rock gardens or raised beds.

Sage doesn't need a lot of maintaining or watering. Later in the year, the plants become straggly but can be cut back to the shape you want them.

Sage flowers can be candied and leaves can be dried. Dry sprigs in a dark airy place, crumble into jars and label. Store out of direct light to help retain the flavour. The leaves can also be frozen.

Sage doesn't tend to like very long cold spells, so is best planted in containers that can be moved into a warmer environment if you have cold winters. In moderate climates sage can be available all year round. Sheltered raised beds or rock garden areas will help keep a fresh supply of leaves even during the coldest months.

Eating sage

Sage isn't a cure-all but does have important healing properties and a glass of sage tea every day will give the system a boost.

- Add a chopped leaf or two to rissoles, burgers or vegetable croquettes.
- Mix with other herbs, such as basil and thyme, and use in stews and casseroles.

Sage and Onion Stuffing

There's nothing like making it yourself!

Ingredients:

4 medium-sized onions, peeled and left whole
10 sage leaves
5 oz (125 g) breadcrumbs
1 ½ oz (40 g) unsalted butter, softened
1 egg yolk
Seasoning

Method:

1. Put the whole onions in a large pan of water and bring to the boil.
2. Reduce heat and simmer for about 10 minutes, adding the sage leaves during the last couple of minutes of cooking time. Don't add them before as the taste of sage can be very strong if cooked for too long.
3. Drain well and put onions and sage in a mixing bowl. Chop finely and stir well together.
4. Add breadcrumbs, softened butter and seasoning and mix together well.
5. Bind together with an egg yolk and use to stuff a chicken or shape into balls ready for baking.

Sage is a very strong tasting herb and should be used sparingly. Too much can make food taste bitter.

HOUSEHOLD TIPS

- Sage is a natural anti-septic and will aid in the healing of minor cuts and grazes. At certain times in history sage has been known as a 'cure-all' but it has always been recognised as an important healing herb.
- A cup of sage tea every day will blow away the cobwebs and make you feel good. It is also effective in reducing menopausal symptoms such as hot flushes.

THYME

About thyme

Thyme has played a part in everyday family life for many centuries and has many myths and legends surrounding it. Once it was believed that if a woman wore a sprig of thyme behind her ear she would attract a husband. Nowadays we tend to just throw it in the pot and cook a nice meal!

Thyme is used in many medicinal preparations to help alleviate cold and flu symptoms, and is very effective. It has been cultivated for medicinal and culinary use for hundreds of years and is considered to be a good preservative for meat.

Thyme is a hardy perennial and will grace your herb garden for many years. It originates from Mediterranean areas and will tolerate very dry conditions. Thyme has an unmistakeable sweet smell and is a good herb to grow in containers on a patio where the leaves are brushed against to release the scent.

Growing thyme

Growing thyme from seed is very satisfying but it will be a while before you can use it. Seed can be sown early in the year in well-drained trays or pots of compost and kept inside or in a greenhouse until the plants are large enough to handle, and all danger of frost has passed.

The seed can also be sown outside from around May onwards. Sow thinly as the plants will need space when they come up. Thin seedlings to allow around 2 ft (60 cm) of space for each plant. Don't use any leaves in the first year though.

Thyme can also be propagated from cuttings or root division. To start from cuttings, take 3–4 inch (8–10 cm) cuttings from a healthy established plant and push them, cut side down, into pots of fresh compost. Make sure the pots are well drained and watered regularly. Compost shouldn't be too wet though. Keep in a warm sunny spot or indoors until the plants start to grow. In the following spring, cuttings that have developed roots can be transplanted.

Every three or four years, thyme becomes straggly and should be divided. Dig the whole plant up carefully to avoid damaging the roots. Pull the roots apart gently and re-plant the healthiest pieces into pots or containers, or directly into the herb garden.

Position thyme in a sunny spot and water occasionally but never allow it to become too wet. In very cold winters, mulch to protect the roots from freezing.

Thyme is best eaten fresh and will stay green practically all year round, especially if you keep a pot going on a windowsill indoors. It can be dried by hanging stems upside down in a dark airy place then storing in a sealed jar. Label and keep out of direct light. Whole stems can be frozen. Pick before flowers appear and freeze quickly.

Thyme works well as a container herb and is an ideal plant to grow in hanging baskets. Always make sure containers and pots are well drained. Native to Mediterranean areas it likes a sunny spot and doesn't need too much water. Water regularly but don't allow the compost to get too wet.

Bring pots in at the end of the summer to encourage a little more growth.

Eating thyme

Thyme is slow to release its flavour and should be added early in the cooking time.

- Put a couple of whole fresh sprigs in the roasting tin when cooking a joint of lamb or a chicken.
- The tiny thyme leaves can be mixed into burger and rissole mixtures before cooking.
- Sprinkle a few in the salad bowl or use as a garnish for green salads and cold tomato dishes.
- Add to casseroles, soups and stews, and include a sprig of thyme when bunching together herbs for a *bouquet garni* mix.

Thyme is a useful herb to have in the kitchen and enhances the taste of fish and chicken as well as vegetarian dishes.

HOUSEHOLD TIPS

- Thyme is another strong anti-septic and is effective in treating minor wounds. It has been recognised as a soothing herb, and a pillow of thyme can encourage a good night's sleep.
- Thyme has expectorant qualities and is an excellent herb to infuse and drink as a tea at the onset of a cold or a cough. Pour boiling water over a few sprigs of thyme in a jug, cover and leave for five minutes. Strain into a cup or glass and add a spoonful of honey to taste.

CHAPTER 5

FRUITY TREATS

Apples and pears have been grown in British gardens for many years, but traditionally in the form of huge trees that overshadowed the rest of the garden. There are practical hybrid varieties available now that will stay fairly small. Many apple and pear trees will be grafted and although this can be done at home, a certain amount of expertise is required to get it right. Dwarf apple and pear trees can be grown very successfully in a small space and it is worth browsing the varieties available in your local garden centre to decide which ones are best for you.

This chapter concentrates on growing soft fruits as well as lemons. Although lemons originate from Mediterranean areas, oranges and lemons have been grown in hothouses for many years in the UK. The Victorians prided themselves on their orangeries where they grew oranges, lemons and limes. These were, however, mostly connected to wealthy houses as it took an army of gardeners to produce the fruits.

Lemon trees have become very popular over the last few years right across Europe. New hybrid varieties will produce lemons without having to be kept in hothouses, although a certain amount of care is needed to produce a good crop.

This chapter covers five everyday fruits:

- strawberries
- blackberries
- blackcurrants
- raspberries
- lemons.

All of these fruits will grow happily outdoors in the UK climate, although lemons are best grown in containers so that they may be brought indoors during the winter months.

Blackberries grow wild in many parts and can be collected and eaten, although they shouldn't be collected from certain areas (see page 138). New thorn-less varieties are available that are not quite as hardy as the original bramble but are more practical in a smaller garden.

Strawberries, raspberries and blackcurrants have been favourite garden fruits for many generations and you don't need a Ph.D. in botany to grow them. But they will get you lots of brownie points!

STRAWBERRIES

About strawberries

Wild strawberries have been around for thousands of years over many parts of the world. The cultivated strawberry is much sweeter and wild strawberries are rarely collected these days, although they are useful for cooking. Cultivated strawberries first came to the home garden around the sixteenth century and symbolised sweetness and purity. It was once believed that if two sweethearts each ate half of a heart-shaped strawberry, they would fall deeply in love.

Strawberries are easy to grow at home and can be grown in special strawberry planters or any other suitable container, as well as directly outside. There are varieties that will crop more than once a year.

Properties of strawberries

Strawberries are rich in vitamins, in particular vitamin C, and have long been used as a healing herb as well as a special treat in cakes and desserts. They also contain dietary fibre. Strawberry leaf tea is available in health food shops and is a well-established healthy addition to the diet.

Strawberries have been said to cure many ailments including kidney conditions and throat infections. They contain phenol which is an anti-inflammatory and they have been found to be an effective treatment for asthma and rheumatoid arthritis.

Growing strawberries

There are many different varieties of strawberry, including seasonal varieties, which means that with a little careful planning you will be able to grow a couple of different varieties and be harvesting fruit for a long period throughout the year.

Choose a type that produces lots of smaller fruits if you have children. The larger ones will take longer to grow and ripen and, as kids love to pick and eat strawberries, you may as well grow as many as you can.

Don't attempt to start your strawberry bed from wild plants. They are unlikely to produce sweet fruits and will stay very small. The best way to start is to beg some spare plants from a local grower. Every year strawberries put out runners and produce new plants, so there may be some available from a neighbouring gardener. Alternatively, local garden centres usually have a good choice of healthy plants.

A strawberry bed should ideally be moved every few years but you need to find a semi-permanent patch in full sun to get them going. They shouldn't be planted in the same soil that has grown tomatoes, potatoes or peppers in the previous few years. These vegetables can leave a virus in the ground that can damage strawberry plants.

In the autumn before spring plantings dig over the ground and incorporate plenty of well-rotted manure or compost. Remove any perennial weeds and non-organic debris. In the following spring, the ground will need just a light dig and raking over. Strawberry plants grow rather straggly and it's a good idea to place bricks or wood around the bed to keep the plants contained and also to help with maintenance. Don't make the bed too wide. You want to be able to reach the middle from both sides.

Plant strawberry plants so that the roots are covered but not the 'crown'. Allow around 12 in (30 cm) between plants and 18 in (45 cm) between rows. This is a general guide. Check on any special variations when you buy your plants. Water them well after planting.

Although strawberries are a popular fruit to grow at home, there are conflicting ideas about caring for them. Some growers believe you should pick off all the flowers in the first year so that the plants become established and produce strong root growth. The best way is to go with your instincts and advice from growers in your area.

Generally, strawberry plants must be watered regularly and kept weed free. In hot sun, the soil can dry out quickly so a mulch is useful during the summer months. A mulch of straw will help deter slugs as well. As soon as the fruits appear they are vulnerable to slug and bird attacks. The straw will help deter the slugs but bird-friendly netting may be necessary to stop the birds eating all your fruit.

Strawberry plants can be damaged by extreme cold and should be protected during the winter with a cloche or other protection.

The 'mother' plants will send off runners during the growing season. These can be cut from the plant in autumn and re-planted to extend your strawberry bed, or to start a new one. These new baby plants will root themselves if they can and may be left if you wish but the bed will get untidy. Also fruits need space to develop so don't let the strawberry bed become too overcrowded.

Pick strawberries as soon as they are ripe. Don't leave them to rot on the plants.

Strawberries make great patio container plants and specially designed strawberry planters are available at most good garden centres, or online.

Planters should come with manufacturer's guidelines for getting the most from your crops.

Generally, containers should be in a sunny position and watered regularly. Tidy up runners at the end of the season and start another container with them. Strawberries will grow in home-made containers just as well, as long as they are well-drained and looked after.

Eating strawberries

Strawberries are best eaten fresh straight off the plant, or chilled for ten minutes or so in the fridge. Top with double or whipped cream and garnish with a mint leaf or two for an elegant Sunday afternoon tea!

Strawberry Jam

If your strawberry bed takes off and you have more strawberries than you know what to do with, make jam! Store a couple of jars and enjoy the taste of summer through the winter months.

This recipe will make about 5 lbs (2.3 kgs) of jam. Prepare jars in advance: wash thoroughly then dry in the oven, set on the lowest temperature.

Ingredients:
3 lbs (1.4 kg) strawberries
3 lbs (1.4 kg) sugar
Juice of half a lemon

Method:
1. Prepare strawberries: remove leaves, stalks and damaged fruit. Cut into halves. Rinse under slow running water and drain well.
2. Put strawberries and the juice of half a lemon into a heavy-based saucepan.
3. Stir over a medium heat and bring to the boil.
4. Reduce heat and simmer for about 20 minutes or until fruit is soft, stirring all the time to prevent sticking.
5. Remove from heat and stir in the sugar. Stir until all sugar has dissolved.
6. Return to the heat and boil rapidly for 20 minutes.
7. Test for a setting point: Either use a sugar thermometer which should read 221°F, 105°C, or if you haven't got a sugar thermometer available, drop a little jam on to a cold saucer and wait for a few seconds. Rub gently with thumb (be careful, it will be hot). If the surface of the jam wrinkles, it has reached setting point. If not, cook for a few more minutes and test again.

8. Pour carefully into warmed jars. **NB:** Don't pour hot jam into cold glass jars. They will crack easily.
9. Seal and label jars and store out of direct light.

Strawberry Pie or Crumble

Choose between pastry or crumble mix – or make both!

Ingredients:
Enough strawberries to half fill an ovenproof dish
Short-crust pastry, bought or homemade (see tomato quiche, page 8 for short-crust pastry recipe)
A little beaten egg or milk

Or crumble mixture made from:
4–5oz (100–125 g) flour
2oz (50 g) hard butter or margarine, cut into small cubes
2oz (50 g) sugar

Method:
1. Preheat oven to gas mark 4 (350°F, 180°C).
2. Prepare fruit by removing any leaves, stalks and damaged fruit. Cut into halves or quarters if using large strawberries. Rinse gently and drain well.
3. Lay in an ovenproof dish and add a little water to moisten the dish and prevent sticking.
4. Cover dish with pastry and brush a little beaten egg or milk over the top.
5. Or make a crumble mix by rubbing butter into flour until mixture resembles breadcrumbs, adding a little more flour if too sticky. Stir in sugar and pile mix on top of fruit.
6. Bake in the centre of pre-heated oven for about half an hour or until top is starting to go golden brown. Don't over-cook.
7. Serve hot with custard or cream.

OTHER STRAWBERRY IDEAS

- Use to decorate and fill sponge cakes. Cut strawberries in half and lay on the cream or jam filling, then place the other layer of cake on top. After dusting with icing sugar, arrange a few halved strawberries and mint leaves on top.

- Add some to muesli or any other breakfast cereal. A few strawberries in the morning is a healthy way to start your 5-a-day fruit and veg. Use a juicer or blender and add a couple of strawberries to a banana smoothie or a milkshake.

- Mix a few strawberries, cut in half or quarters, into a fruit salad or top your favourite dessert with some.

BLACKBERRIES

About blackberries

Blackberry plants, or brambles as they are commonly known, have been growing wild over many parts of Europe for hundreds if not thousands of years. With the reduction in hedgerows and the fact that there is generally less countryside to go around, the bramble is now often grown as a hybrid in the home garden.

Wild blackberries can be collected, but care should be taken. Don't collect blackberries from the side of the road as they can absorb car pollution. They are also susceptible to chemical sprays and therefore shouldn't be collected from areas near to farmland unless the farm is definitely organic. Also, dogs can pollute low growing fruit. But even taking all those factors into account, there are blackberries from the wild that can still be harvested.

The hybrids available for home growing are less hardy than the original wild bramble, but they take up less space and as a bonus many of them are thorn-less.

Properties of blackberries

Blackberry fruits and leaves have a high vitamin and mineral content. The fruits are high in vitamin C and the leaves have been used as a medicinal aid for many years. They effectively alleviate symptoms of diarrhoea and other stomach problems. They are also said to help soothe mouth ulcers. Blackberry is a good tonic and a cup of blackberry leaf tea every day will help boost the immune system and prevent colds and flu bugs.

The fruits and leaves also contain anti-oxidants which help fight against free radicals therefore preventing some cancers and heart disease.

Growing blackberries

Anyone who has ever taken over a neglected garden or piece of land will know that brambles aren't to be messed with! If you're facing a bramble patch that needs to be sorted, it's tempting to plough the whole lot up – or preferably dynamite it. However, brambles are very hardy plants and if you have a few that could be left and trained to grow where you want them, it's a good idea to tackle them by hand. Arm yourself with a strong pair of shears and protective clothing before you start.

For most of us wanting to grow a few blackberries in the garden, a wild bramble patch isn't an option. Blackberry plants can be grown from seed but will take a long time of looking after before they germinate. The best way to propagate a blackberry patch is either to buy hybrids from a local garden supplier or start your plants using cuttings or by the layering method.

Take cuttings from a healthy plant after the fruit has finished in the autumn. Push cuttings into compost in a seed bed, pots or containers and keep an eye on them until the following spring when roots should have developed. They will then be ready to plant out in their final position. Blackberries are one of the few fruits that will mature in the shade, so if all the sunny spots are taken blackberries can fill a shady spot in your garden.

If the plants have some sun though, they will develop larger fruits and they may be slightly sweeter. Choose your spot carefully if you are planting hybrids. These should come with growing recommendations when you buy them. The area must be well drained. Never plant blackberry canes in waterlogged soil. The soil should be kept moist, so water regularly if they are getting a lot of sun.

Blackberries can also be layered. As with many plants with woody stems, blackberries will produce roots from the stem. Choose a healthy lower branch from a well-established plant and peg to the ground with a V-shaped peg where it naturally touches the soil. Water regularly. Mulch during cold weather and by the following spring it should be developing roots.

When new cuttings or layered plants have developed roots, they can be planted out. However, if a long hot summer is expected it may be better to leave them until the following autumn. Keep them watered.

Allow about 18 in (45 cm) between plants when you plant your new canes out. Generally plants started from a hardy rootstock won't need much watering or any other attention, but hybrid varieties may need a little extra care.

Harvest fruits when they are fully black and fall off the stem at a touch. They will keep for a few days in the fridge, but are better eaten on the same day as picking. After fruits have finished, plants can be pruned and new cuttings taken. Most blackberry types will survive very low temperatures but if you are concerned for your variety, mulch with grass cuttings or straw over the winter, remembering to remove any un-rotted material early in the spring to aerate the soil.

Blackberries are originally a wild outdoor plant and not really suitable for container growing. However, new hybrid varieties are available now that could be grown successfully in containers. Check on manufacturer's growing recommendations to get the most from your plants.

Eating blackberries

Collecting blackberries with the kids always has an air of anticipation about it. If you can persuade them not to eat too many while they are picking, they will look forward to a blackberry and apple crumble without a doubt.

Blackberry and Apple Crumble

You don't have to put apples with blackberries but they really are delicious together and a traditional English teatime recipe.

Ingredients:
2 large cooking apples or 3–4 dessert apples
Enough blackberries to fill about a third of an ovenproof dish
A little sugar

Crumble mixture made from:
4–5oz (100–125 g) flour
2oz (50 g) hard butter or margarine, cut into small cubes
2oz (50 g) sugar

Method:
1. Preheat oven to gas mark 4 (350°F, 180°C).
2. Peel and core apples and cut into thin slices. Put them into a pan with a little water.

3. Bring gently to the boil, then reduce heat and simmer until apples are soft. Cooking apples will take longer to cook than dessert apples. (Some very soft dessert apples may not need any pre-cooking.)
4. Drain apples, reserving the liquid.
5. Lay apples in an ovenproof dish and top with prepared blackberries to fill the dish to half or two-thirds full.
6. Sprinkle a little sugar over the fruit and then pour over a couple of tablespoons of the reserved liquid from the cooking apples, or use water.
7. Make crumble mix by rubbing butter into flour until mixture resembles breadcrumbs, adding a little more flour if too sticky. Stir in sugar and pile mix on top of fruit.
8. Bake in the centre of pre-heated oven for about half an hour or until top is starting to go golden brown. Don't over-cook.
9. Serve hot or cold with custard or cream.

Blackberry Tarts and Pies

Blackberries are a very soft fruit that need little cooking so are ideal for making 'jam' tarts. Pastry lids turn tarts into individual blackberry pies.

Ingredients:
Short-crust pastry, bought or homemade (see tomato quiche, page 8 for short-crust pastry recipe)
Blackberries
A little sugar
Pies need to be baked 'blind' with greaseproof paper and dried beans
A little beaten egg or milk to glaze (optional)

Method:
1. Preheat oven to gas mark 5 (375°F, 190°C).
2. Make pastry, roll out thinly and line lightly greased patty tins. Prick pastry gently with a fork.

3. For individual tarts, mash blackberries and fill pastry cases. Sprinkle with a little sugar and bake in the centre of pre-heated oven for about 10–15 minutes.
4. For blackberry pies, line the patty tins with pastry, prick with a fork, then bake 'blind' for 5–10 minutes until pastry is set. To bake 'blind': Cover pastry with a layer of greaseproof paper and then a layer or two of dried beans.
5. Remove from the oven but don't turn the oven off. Remove beans and greaseproof paper from pastry. Spoon mashed blackberries into pastry cases and sprinkle a little sugar over. Put a smaller circle of pastry over the top of the fruit.
6. The top can be brushed with a little beaten egg or milk to glaze.
7. Cook in the centre of a pre-heated oven for 10–15 minutes until tops are golden brown. Remove from heat and sprinkle a little sugar over the pies, if liked, while still hot. Cool on a wire rack.

Blackberry and Apple Jam

Another delicious blackberry and apple combination. This recipe will make about 5 lbs (2.3 kgs) of jam. Prepare jars in advance: wash thoroughly then dry in the oven, set to the lowest temperature.

Ingredients:
2 lbs (0.9 kg) blackberries
12 oz (350 g) cooking apples
3 lbs (1.4 kg) sugar
6 fl oz (150 mls) water

Method:
1. Remove all leaves and stems from blackberries and rinse gently.
2. Put into a large heavy-based pan with half the water and bring to the boil over a fairly low heat, stirring from time to time to prevent sticking. Reduce heat and simmer until the fruit is soft.
3. Peel, core and slice apples and put them into a heavy-based saucepan with the rest of the water. Simmer gently until the apples are soft.

4. Mash the apples with a wooden spoon or a potato masher, then stir in the blackberries.
5. Add the sugar to the apple and blackberry pulp while still hot and stir until dissolved.
6. Bring to the boil and boil fairly rapidly for about 10 minutes, stirring often.
7. Test for setting point: Either use a sugar thermometer which should read 221°F, 105°C, or if you haven't got a sugar thermometer available, drop a little jam on to a cold saucer and wait for a few seconds. Rub gently with thumb (be careful, it will be hot). If the surface of the jam wrinkles, it has reached setting point. If not, cook for a few more minutes and test again.
8. Pour carefully into warmed jars. **NB:** Don't pour hot jam into cold glass jars. They will crack easily.
9. Seal and label jars and store out of direct light.

OTHER BLACKBERRY IDEAS

Blackberries can also be added to:

- fruit salads
- ice cream desserts
- yoghurts
- smoothies.

Blackberries are a popular ingredient in wine making and are often used with grapes or on their own to produce a country wine.

BLACKCURRANTS

About blackcurrants

Blackcurrants must be one of the world's most commercially grown crops. They are widely used in alcoholic beverages and the juice has been a favourite cordial for children and adults for many years.

Blackcurrants have been picked in the wild for probably thousands of years and used in medicinal preparations since the Middle Ages. It wasn't until the nineteenth and twentieth centuries that research uncovered just how power packed this simple little fruit is. With high quantities of vitamin C it is probably one of the best garden fruits to grow. Bushes take up relatively little space and are hardy perennials, making them a good crop to grow in less than warm climates.

Properties of blackcurrants

During the Second World War vitamin C was hard to come by and farmers and households alike were encouraged to grow as many blackcurrants as possible. Practically the whole farmed crop of blackcurrants at that time was used to make cordials and British children have been drinking it ever since.

Blackcurrants are also a good source of calcium, iron and protein.

Growing blackcurrants

Blackcurrants are propagated from canes (cuttings) from established and healthy plants. They like a sunny position but will tolerate some shade if necessary.

Although the blackcurrant plant is a hardy perennial, and will cope with most soil types, the ground must be well drained. It's a good idea to do a little preparation before planting. Dig over the area and remove any perennial weeds, non-organic debris and large stones, and dig in some well-rotted manure or compost during the autumn before spring plantings.

Hybrid plants are normally available during the winter to early spring from garden suppliers. Choose a variety that requires little maintenance or, alternatively, start your blackcurrants from cuttings.

After harvesting all fruits, take cuttings from a well-established plant and push into a bed or large container of fresh compost. Keep watered but don't allow the soil to become waterlogged. The cuttings should develop roots over the following year and be ready to plant out in the following autumn, or before.

As long as the ground is workable and not too wet or frozen, plant out shop-bought or home produced plants in the garden anytime from autumn to spring. Each plant needs about 6 ft (2 m) of growing room and should be positioned in a sunny spot if possible.

Water plants well and don't allow them to dry out. To keep moisture in the ground, you can apply a mulch. Mulch helps to keep weeds away and moisture in. Use a good quality garden compost as a mulch and you will also be feeding the soil at the same time.

Harvest blackcurrants when they are ready. Don't leave them on the bush for the birds or, worse, let them rot. They should be picked on a dry day where possible, as wet blackcurrants will perish much faster than dry picked ones. If you pick them when they are dry they can be stored in the fridge for a couple of days.

Leave the plants to grow in their first year but prune back in subsequent years after harvesting all the fruits. You may have specific pruning recommendations for your variety of blackcurrant but, generally, use a sharp pair of secateurs and cut away about 20% of the wood from the middle of the plant and a little from the outside, but not too much. Tidy each plant up by cutting out crossed branches. Prune carefully and the plant will last for many years and produce more blackcurrants every season.

Blackcurrants aren't generally suitable for container growing. They don't thrive if their root growth is restricted. They are also better grown outside unless you are in a particularly hard growing region. Possibly near to the coast they will need some protection from the wind. Otherwise blackcurrants are a hardy bush and will last for many years in a home garden.

Eating blackcurrants

As well as the infamous juices and other drinks, blackcurrants can be used in many recipes.

Blackcurrant Jam

This recipe will make about 10 lbs (4.5 kgs) of jam. Prepare jars in advance: wash thoroughly then dry in the oven, set on the lowest temperature.

Ingredients:
4 lbs (1.8 kg) blackcurrants
6 lbs (2.7 k g) sugar
3 pints (1.7 litres) water

Method:
1. Prepare blackcurrants: Remove stalks, leaves and any damaged fruit. Wash under running water and drain.
2. Put the fruit into a heavy-based or preserving pan with the water. Bring to the boil over a medium heat, then reduce heat and simmer for about 45 minutes, stirring regularly to prevent fruit sticking to the pan.
3. Contents of pan should have reduced a little and fruit should be tender.
4. Remove from heat and stir in the sugar.
5. Stir until sugar has dissolved, then return pan to the heat and boil rapidly for about 10 minutes.
6. Test for setting point: Either use a sugar thermometer which should read 221°F, 105°C, or if you haven't got a sugar thermometer available, drop a little jam on to a cold saucer and wait for a few seconds. Rub gently with

thumb (be careful, it will be hot). If the surface of the jam wrinkles, it has reached setting point. If not, cook for a few more minutes and test again.

7. Pour carefully into warmed jars. **NB:** Don't pour hot jam into cold glass jars. They will crack easily.
8. Seal and label jars and store out of direct light.

Blackcurrant Pie

Taste fruit before baking in case it is a little sharp in taste. Add a little more sugar if needed.

Ingredients:
Short-crust pastry, bought or homemade (see tomato quiche, page 8 for short-crust pastry recipe)
1 lb (450 g) blackcurrants
3 oz (75 g) sugar
A little water
A little milk or beaten egg to glaze (optional)

Method:
1. Pre-heat oven to gas mark 6, (400°F, 200°C).
2. Prepare blackcurrants: Remove stalks, leaves and wash under gently running water. Drain.
3. Put about half the blackcurrants into an ovenproof dish with a little water to prevent fruit sticking to dish.
4. Sprinkle over the sugar and put the rest of the fruit into dish.
5. Cover with bought or homemade pastry and glaze with a little beaten egg or milk.
6. Bake in the centre of pre-heated oven for about 45 minutes. The top of the dish can be covered loosely with silver foil to prevent over-browning.
7. Serve hot with custard or cold with cream or ice cream.

MORE BLACKCURRANT IDEAS

- Make your own blackcurrant juice. Clean the fruit, add water and bring to the boil. Reduce the heat and simmer until the fruit is soft. Allow to cool and blend in a food processor or liquidiser, adding more water if a more diluted juice is required. Add a little lemon juice or honey according to taste or simply leave it natural. Sugar can be added if blackcurrants aren't sweet enough. Pour into a sterilised bottle and use within a few days.
- Make your own juice then freeze it in ice-lolly moulds – fresh organic blackcurrant ice lollies!
- Cook blackcurrants and mash or blend, then mix with ice cream or cream to make a quick and delicious dessert. Sprinkle with a little sugar if blackcurrants are a little sharp in taste.
- Add a few to fruit salads.

Blackcurrants can be kept for a few days in the fridge, as long as they are dry when picked and unwashed before storing. It is possible to freeze them, but some texture and taste will be lost. They are better used in recipes before freezing.

RASPBERRIES

About raspberries

It is believed that raspberries have been available across many parts of the world since prehistoric times. It wasn't until the sixteenth century that they were cultivated and different strains were recorded from the eighteenth century.

There are many different varieties of raspberry that can be grown in the home garden. The plants take up little space and can be grown as a border. Your local garden supplier should have different varieties available, including golden and purple raspberries.

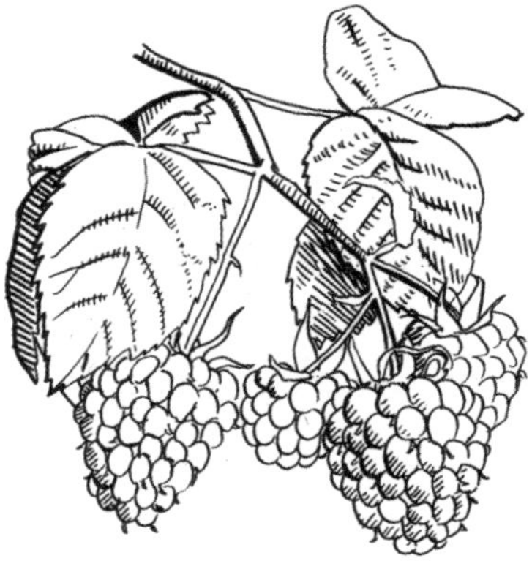

Raspberries have always been considered to be a healthy food and are a good source of vitamins. Because they are a soft fruit and don't travel well, they are often expensive to buy, which makes them even more attractive to grow at home.

Properties of raspberries

Raspberries are a good source of dietary fibre, having 6.5 g of fibre per 100 g, as well as being rich in vitamins and minerals. They contain around 50% more antioxidants than strawberries and help fight against cell damaging diseases.

Raspberries have a high vitamin C content as well as a significant amount of vitamin E, not always found in fruits and vegetables. They lose about half their vitamin C content in freezing, so should be eaten fresh wherever possible.

Growing raspberries

Before you buy raspberry canes, browse through a catalogue or two as there are many new and interesting varieties available from most garden suppliers.

Buy healthy canes that have well-developed roots or start off your own plants from cuttings. Take cuttings from a well-established plant after all the fruit has been harvested and push the cuttings, cut end down, into a large pot or seedbed of fresh compost. Keep weed free and watered until the following autumn, when roots should have developed. Start as many cuttings as you can because not all of them may be successful.

Raspberries, like most soft fruits, prefer a sunny spot in the garden. They are a hardy plant and will produce fruit in a partially shady spot but the fruits may not develop as well as those growing in full sun.

Prepare the ground by digging over and removing any perennial weeds and non-organic debris. Make sure the soil is well drained. Incorporate some sand or very light gravel to help with drainage if necessary. Plant your canes or rooted cuttings in the autumn to winter months. Raspberry canes can be planted in the spring as well, but are unlikely to produce much fruit during the first year.

Dig a trench for the canes and plant them about 12–18 in (30–45 cm) apart along the row and leave about 2–3 ft (60–90 cm) between rows. Some varieties of raspberry will benefit from a support system. Check on the growing recommendations before you plant for variations on spacing and any advice on supporting the plants.

Plant canes in the trench and fill with fresh rich compost. Heel the canes in firmly and water well. If a very cold winter is expected, it is advisable to mulch around the new canes for the first year to prevent damage to the new roots.

With a sharp pair of secateurs, cut canes down to about 10–12 in (25–30 cm) straight after planting to encourage growth. In the following spring after planting, new suckers may appear which can be removed and re-planted. The new suckers should be transplanted every year to avoid overcrowding.

Mulch during the spring with organic material. In the summer, cut the original cane down to the ground and let the new branches produce the fruit. Raspberries fruit on new wood every year. After harvesting, the old wood should be removed, new suckers transplanted and then the remaining canes should be mulched for the winter months. Raspberries are heavy feeders and will benefit from a good organic feed from time to time.

Most raspberries are hardy and won't need any other protection in the cold weather. Check on your particular variety before planting but generally they don't need valuable polytunnel or indoor space.

Don't let your raspberry canes dry out but make sure the area is well drained.

Raspberries are not particularly suitable for container growing as the roots need a large area to spread, and some varieties grow tall and will need support that isn't always practical in a container.

Eating raspberries

Raspberries are best eaten fresh on the day you pick them, but will keep for a day or two in the fridge. They can be frozen but will lose some of the texture and taste. Freeze quickly if you want to keep some for the winter.

Raspberries are very soft and can be easily mashed to a puree and mixed with rice puddings, ice cream or made into fruit tartlets. To make individual tartlets, see the recipe for blackberry pies and tarts (page 142) and replace blackberries with raspberries.

Raspberry Meringue

This is an extra special Sunday treat!

Ingredients:
12 oz (375 g) fresh raspberries
6 oz (150 g) caster sugar
3 egg whites
10 oz (300 mls) whipping cream
Greaseproof paper

Method:

1. Pre-heat oven to gas mark ¼ (225°F, 110°C).
2. Cut an 8 in (20 cm) circle of greaseproof paper and place on a baking sheet.
3. Whisk egg whites until stiff.
4. Add half the sugar to the egg whites, a little at a time, beating well after each addition.

5. Fold in the rest of the sugar gently using a metal spoon.
6. Spread some of the mixture over the circle of greaseproof paper, then make a thick rim around the edge of the circle to form a case.
7. Bake in the centre of pre-heated oven for 2½–3 hours until set but still white. If meringue starts to brown before it has set properly, leave the oven door open a little.
8. Remove from the oven and leave to cool.
9. Prepare the raspberries: Remove any leaves, stems and damaged fruit, rinse gently under very slowly running water if needed then drain well.
10. When meringue case is completely cold, put the raspberries in the middle then whip the cream and pile on top of the fruit.

Raspberry Jam

If you have more raspberries than you can possibly eat, a pot or two of raspberry jam is a wonderful store cupboard ingredient.

This recipe will make about 6.5 lbs (3 kgs) of jam. Prepare jars in advance: wash thoroughly then dry in the oven, set on the lowest temperature.

Ingredients:
4 lbs (1.8 kg) fresh raspberries
4 lbs (1.8 kg) sugar

Method:
1. Prepare fruit: remove any leaves, stalks and damaged fruit. Rinse gently and drain.
2. Put fruit into a large heavy-based saucepan or preserving pan.
3. Bring to the boil, then lower the heat and simmer for about 20 minutes, stirring from time to time to prevent sticking.
4. Make sure the fruit is very soft, then remove from the heat and stir in the sugar. Keep stirring until sugar has dissolved.
5. Return to the heat and boil rapidly for about 30 minutes.

6. Test for setting point: Either use a sugar thermometer which should read 221°F, 105°C, or if you haven't got a sugar thermometer available, drop a little jam on to a cold saucer and wait for a few seconds. Rub gently with thumb (be careful, it will be hot). If the surface of the jam wrinkles, it has reached setting point. If not, cook for a few more minutes and test again.
7. Leave to stand for 15 minutes then remove any scum from the surface of the jam.
8. Spoon carefully into warmed jars. **NB:** Don't pour hot jam into cold glass jars. They will crack easily.
9. Seal and label jars and store out of direct light.

MORE RASPBERRY IDEAS

- Add a few raspberries to breakfast cereals or yoghurts.
- Stir raspberries gently into a fruit salad.
- Make smoothies and mix with other berries or bananas.
- Puree raspberries to mix into ice cream or any other favourite dessert.

LEMONS

About lemons

Lemons, along with other citrus fruits such as oranges and limes, are indigenous to warmer climates. In Victorian times in England, the rich grew their own citrus fruits in large orangeries staffed by an army of gardeners. The individual fruits worked out to be very expensive.

In recent years, lemons have become a popular shrub in many parts of the world and although they need a little attention, new hybrid varieties make it a lot easier to harvest your own lemons, even if you don't live in the Mediterranean.

There are a number of different lemons you can grow, and they are worth their weight in gold, especially when it comes to adding a slice to your favourite drink!

Properties of lemons

One peeled lemon weighing approximately 58 grams contains around 30 mg of vitamin C. Lemons are low in calories and also are a source of dietary fibre. They are used in many medicinal preparations, and have been for generations. The most well known is probably lemon and honey which is a perfect combination for soothing symptoms of colds and flu.

Lemons are also employed in cleaning products because of their grease-cutting properties. Lemon juice has also been used as a bleaching agent for hair colouring and at one time was thought to remove freckles if dabbed on gently. However, there is little scientific evidence to support this as being a healthy cosmetic exercise, particularly as lemon juice will dry the skin.

Growing lemons

Lemons need a warm sunny spot and won't survive temperatures of less than −1°C or 30°F. Always protect against cold weather either by wrapping a nice warm blanket around them or preferably growing in a large container that can be brought inside during the winter.

Generally lemons are grown in containers in the UK and similar climates. They need a sunny spot when they are outside during the summer. Lemon trees make attractive and practical patio container plants.

Choose a healthy plant from your local garden supplier and check through the manufacturer's growing recommendations before you start as different hybrid varieties may have different requirements.

If you are growing your lemon tree in a container it should be large enough to accommodate the tree's growth but it also needs to be transportable so that you can wheel it inside during the winter. There are trolleys you can buy for moving large containers. Prepare in advance so you don't strain your muscles trying to move an awkward and heavy pot.

Growing lemon trees outside needs careful planning. The tree must be planted in a warm sunny spot out of wind tunnels and it must never be planted in a frost pocket or waterlogged soil. Choose a well-drained sunny spot and dig a large hole before planting. Plant your tree and fill with rich well-rotted manure or compost. Water the tree in well.

All lemons, whether container grown or out in the garden, need watering about once a week. Don't be tempted to water a little every day. They prefer to have a good drink once a week and then be left. To get water to the roots faster, sink a plastic bottle with the bottom cut off into the ground next to your lemon plant. Leave the cap on the bottle, unscrew and water well once a week, then screw the cap back on to prevent the bottle getting clogged with leaves or stones.

Some growers believe you should pick off the young immature fruits as they appear for the first two years. This is painful, when you really want your lemons to develop, but it can help to strengthen the plant for better harvests in subsequent years.

There are a number of new resistant strains of lemon trees available but there are a few pests and diseases to which lemons are susceptible, so watch out for any mould, aphids or leaves dropping. If treated quickly, most problems can be cleared up and your tree will go on to live a full life!

Bring indoors during the cold weather and always put out in the warm sun when the weather improves and your lemon tree will thrive.

Generally in the UK and across the world where winters are cold, lemons are grown in containers so that they may be easily transported inside during the colder months of the year.

Use large well-drained containers, and position in a sunny spot in the garden while the weather is warm. Don't leave plants out on cold nights, and water about once a week.

Check on manufacturer's growing recommendations to get the most from your plants.

Eating lemons

Lemons are one of those kitchen ingredients, like garlic, that no good chef would be without. Even if you don't consider yourself to be a particularly good chef, a little lemon juice in the right places can win you lots of brownie points in the kitchen.

HOMEMADE LEMONADE

This is a quick recipe that you can make at home. No fizz though! Roughly chop three whole (unwaxed) lemons and put them into a food processor with around 6 oz (150 g) of caster sugar and 1 pt (0.5 l) of cold water. Blend until the lemons are finely chopped. Sieve into a large bowl, pressing as much juice as you can through the sieve. Top up with another pint of water and serve. Chill or add ice cubes.

Lemon Meringue Pie

This recipe is probably one of the more well-known lemon desserts although there are plenty more.

Ingredients:

6 oz (150 g) short-crust pastry, bought or homemade (for homemade recipe, see quiche on page 8)
4 oz (100 g) granulated sugar
3 oz (75 g) cornflour
6 tablespoons (90 mls) water
Finely grated rind and juice of 2 lemons
2 eggs, separated
3 oz (75 g) caster sugar

Greaseproof paper and dried beans for baking 'blind'

Method:

Pastry case:

1. Pre-heat oven to gas mark 6 (400°F, 200°C).
2. Roll out pastry to fit an 8 in (20 cm) tin.
3. Lightly grease the tin and line with the pastry. Chill for 30 minutes.
4. Cover pastry with greaseproof paper and pile beans on top. Bake in pre-heated oven for about 15 minutes.
5. Remove from the oven, take out beans and greaseproof paper and put back in the oven for 5 mins to set.
6. Remove from the oven and set aside.
7. Reduce oven heat to gas mark 2 (300°F, 150°C) for the meringue.

Lemon filling:

1. Put the grated rind and juice of the 2 lemons in a heavy-based saucepan with the granulated sugar.
2. Heat gently, stirring until sugar has dissolved.
3. In a small bowl, mix cornflour with water to form a smooth paste.

4. Stir paste into lemon mixture.
5. Bring mixture to the boil, stirring well, and boil for about a minute until the mixture thickens.
6. Remove from heat and leave to cool for a few minutes.
7. Beat in 2 egg yolks, one at a time, then pour mixture into pastry case, levelling off with a palette knife.

Meringue:

1. Whisk the 2 egg whites until stiff then whisk in half the caster sugar until well mixed.
2. Gently fold in the other half of the caster sugar.
3. Spoon on to the lemon filling and smooth over with a palette knife, or flick meringue up into peaks with the point of a knife.
4. Bake for about 35 minutes in pre-heated oven. Serve hot or cold.

Mediterranean Potatoes

Although this is traditionally a potato dish, the taste of the lemon juice really brings the dish alive!

Ingredients:

3 or 4 medium-sized peeled potatoes, cut into cubes
1 sweet pepper
1 courgette
1 medium onion
Juice of 1 lemon
A little olive or nut oil
Handful of chopped fresh herbs (optional)

Method:

1. Boil or steam the potatoes until just cooked. Drain and set aside.
2. Slice courgette, pepper and onion and fry gently in a little oil for a few minutes until tender.

3. Stir in cooked potatoes and herbs if using and fry gently for a few more minutes until all vegetables are hot right through.
4. Add lemon juice to the pan. Stir carefully and cook for a further minute.
5. Serve hot.

MORE LEMON IDEAS

- Cut lemons into wedges and serve with all fish dishes.
- Squeeze lemon juice on salads and other green vegetables.
- Add a slice to your favourite drink. A slice of lemon in a glass of water makes those eight glasses of water a day a lot more enjoyable.
- Squeeze a little lemon juice on cut apples to stop them going brown before cooking. This is really helpful if you are preparing a lot of windfall apples for a pie.
- Make a homemade lemon sorbet.

Lemons look very attractive in a fruit bowl but remember to use them in the kitchen as often as possible.

HOUSEHOLD TIPS

- Keep bits of lemon to rub around sinks and other kitchen work surfaces. The lemon juice will help remove grease and can save you having to buy kitchen detergents. Rinse over lightly after using to remove any sticky residue. The kitchen will smell delicious!

CHAPTER 6

DELICIOUS BLOOMS

Flowers have been used as decoration for thousands of years – in the home, wedding and christening celebrations and as a garnish for food. Flowers are not only decorative, many of them are a good source of nutrition and can be eaten and enjoyed!

There are, of course, blooms and plants that are highly toxic. But as long as you can recognise the flowers you are growing and using, then there should be no problem. The same applies to fungi. There are some wonderful species of wild fungi that are perfectly safe to eat – but there are others that are extremely dangerous.

Generally the petals of flowers are the best part to consume and it is advisable to remove the parts that join to the stem as these are often quite bitter in taste.

Grow your own edible flowers and garnish everyday meals. It's amazing how a few nasturtium or chive flowers brighten up the plainest green salad, and add a unique taste that the whole family will love!

Never consume flowers picked from the side of the road, or those bought from a florist, unless you are sure they haven't been sprayed with chemicals. They could have high levels of toxins.

This chapter covers five delicious blooms:

- dandelions
- marigolds
- nasturtiums
- roses
- violets.

There are plenty more that can be eaten:

- Courgette flowers are a delicacy. Try them dipped in batter and fried.
- Flowers from chive plants can be added to salads.
- Broccoli flowers are also edible.

Always make certain you know what you are eating as not all flowers are suitable for human consumption.

DANDELIONS

About dandelions

Dandelions are a very strong diuretic and should not be taken internally too close to bedtime! They are also a common weed considered by many gardeners to be a nuisance. However, nature tends to provide what we need and the common dandelion is a very useful plant. Like the lawn daisy, dandelions also have entertainment value. Children love to blow the seed 'clocks', counting each puff to find out what time it is, or whether 'she loves me' or 'she loves me not'.

Dandelions are a versatile plant. If your garden gets over-run with them, treat them as gifts rather than weeds. The flower heads can be used to make jam in place of fruit, the young leaves can be added to the salad bowl and have a high vitamin C content. The root can be roasted and ground to make a very acceptable substitute for coffee and the milky sap inside the stem is an effective cure for warts and verrucas. Every single part of a dandelion plant is useful, which is probably why nature provides them in such abundance!

Growing dandelions

To be honest, dandelions shouldn't need cultivating but if you want to grow a large quantity for jam making, grab some seed and plant in a sunny spot. Keep watered but make sure they are not waterlogged. Dandelions are considered to be weeds by most gardeners and will usually re-seed and come up all over the place.

If, for some reason, dandelions don't come of their own accord in your garden, you may have to look elsewhere and wait for the seed head to appear, after flowering. Only collect from farmer's fields if you can be sure the ground is free of chemicals. And never collect from the side of the road because of car and animal pollution.

It isn't always easy to find dandelion seed for sale, although some specialist seed suppliers may be able to help.

If the plants come up in your vegetable plot, dig up the root and re-plant or throw on the compost heap. Try and catch them when they are small as they have a long tap root and take hold fairly quickly. Don't leave them to grow in

your vegetable patch as they will re-seed and soon take over, drawing valuable nutrients from the soil and depriving your other crops. But if you can leave a couple to produce seed, then you can re-direct them next year.

Generally dandelions will grow in any soil type, even the poorest, but if you can provide a nice fertile sunny spot and look after them for a while, your crop will be better. Dig over a patch beforehand, incorporate some well-rotted manure or fresh compost and remove any large stones and non-organic debris. Rake the ground over to a fine tilth and if you have seed, scatter over the prepared bed and gently tamp down with the back of a rake. Watch that the birds don't find the seeds.

Dandelions will rarely need watering, only in very long dry spells. Their long tap root finds water before other plants will.

Many gardeners will probably think you are crazy growing dandelions on purpose, but most gardeners are slightly crazy themselves anyway, so take no notice! Dandelions are a great plant to grow and should be used as much as possible.

There doesn't seem to be any reason why not to grow dandelions in containers, although they do have a very long tap root. To get the best development from your plants, the container needs to be quite deep, and of course well-drained.

Eating dandelions

You really can use every part of the dandelion plant. The root is commercially grown as a substitute for coffee, and has been used for generations as the main ingredient in dandelion and burdock wines and cordials.

DANDELION GREENS

Dandelion leaves can be eaten like spinach or any spring greens. So if you are ever in the wilderness without food, look for the hardy dandelion to sustain you!

Put washed leaves in a saucepan and just cover with water. Bring to the boil, then reduce the heat and simmer until the leaves are tender. Drain well and chop finely. Serve hot. Dandelion leaves can also be steamed. Add a few chopped fresh herbs, or other seasoning to your taste, during cooking.

If the cooked leaves are bitter, drain well, add fresh water and a small spoonful of sugar and re-cook for a few minutes.

SALAD LEAVES

Use young fresh dandelion leaves in salads. Avoid the older, larger leaves as they tend to taste bitter. Finely slice leaves and toss them into a green salad and add a dressing.

STIR-FRY

Finely sliced leaves can also be added in the last few seconds of cooking a stir-fry. Again only use young leaves.

Dandelion Jam

This old traditional French recipe for dandelion jam requires you to collect 365 dandelion flowers on the first day of the year on which you see them all over the fields and gardens. I tried to double the recipe once and it didn't work, so the 365 bit is important!

This recipe will make a little over 2 lbs (1 kg) of jam. Prepare jars in advance: wash thoroughly then dry in the oven, set on the lowest temperature.

Ingredients:

365 freshly picked dandelion flowers
2 lbs (1 kg) sugar
Grated rind and juice of 2 oranges and 1 lemon

Method:

1. Prepare flowers: remove any leaves, stalks and other greenery from the flowers. Rinse gently and drain.
2. Put into a large heavy-based saucepan or preserving pan with the grated rind and juice of 2 oranges and a lemon.
3. Bring to the boil, then lower the heat and simmer for about 20 minutes, stirring from time to time to prevent sticking.
4. Remove from the heat and stir in the sugar. Keep stirring until sugar has dissolved, then push mixture through a sieve.
5. Return to the heat and boil rapidly for about 30 minutes.
6. Test for setting point: Either use a sugar thermometer which should read 221°F, 105°C, or if you haven't got a sugar thermometer available, drop a little jam on to a cold saucer and wait for a few seconds. Rub gently with thumb (be careful, it will be hot). If the surface of the jam wrinkles, it has reached setting point. If not, cook for a few more minutes and test again.
7. Spoon carefully into warmed jars. **NB:** Don't pour hot jam into cold glass jars. They will crack easily.
8. Seal and label jars and store out of direct light.

DANDELION COFFEE

Scrub dandelion roots and roast until cooked through. Leave to cool and then grind to make a substitute for coffee. Although to coffee drinkers this tastes nothing like coffee and is a poor substitute for the taste, it is a healthy drink as it is full of vitamins and minerals and seriously lacking in caffeine.

HOUSEHOLD TIPS

- The milky sap from a dandelion stem can be a helpful cure for warts and verrucas. This is an old-fashioned remedy worth trying before you head off to the chemist.
- Simply dab the sap directly on to the affected area two or three times a day.

MARIGOLDS

About marigolds

Marigold is easily recognisable and a very popular garden plant. It tends to be fairly hardy and therefore easy to grow. There are many different varieties of marigold, but if you stick to the basic *calendula officinalis* you will be sure of having an edible plant that contains many vitamins and has a great taste.

Calendula officinalis, or pot marigold, is best to use in meals as other varieties have very dense petals, are usually hybrid varieties and can be lacking in vitamins. If you are going to eat a flower, it may as well be a highly nutritious one!

Marigolds have been grown over many centuries as a healing herb to soothe the nerves. They can be infused as a tea or added to soups, as well as mixed in with lotions to help the healing of wounds. The petals will make an effective homemade dye. Marigolds have also been used as a hair tonic.

Growing marigolds

Marigolds like a sunny position and will grow well along borders, in flowerbeds or even dotted about in the vegetable plot.

Sow seeds in well-drained pots or trays of seed compost in early spring. Keep them inside the house or in a greenhouse. Keep the soil damp and warm until the plants are ready to put outside. In warmer climates seed can be sown directly outside in rows. Thin plants when they are a few inches (5–8 cm) high, allowing about 9 in (20–25 cm) of space all round to grow.

Apart from keeping them free of weeds, marigolds shouldn't need any other attention. If the weather is unusually dry, water the plants a little but normally spring is damp and marigolds will thrive on their own in the early months of the year. If you are starting your plants off inside, it is a good idea to water regularly until the plants are ready to be put out in the garden. Keep the compost damp but not too wet.

Although marigolds need little maintenance, watch out for slugs. Protect your plants, especially when they are young, from slugs and snails by any organic method you can find.

Use the flowers as you need them in the kitchen or to brighten up the house with small posies in bowls or vases. Marigolds are a curious plant as they produce many flowering branches from the main flowering stem. Picking regularly seems to encourage more growth and more blooms.

The flowers will bloom right through the summer, coming out in the morning and closing at night. Leave a few flowers to develop on the plants and they will self-seed, giving you a bed full of beautiful orange flowers next year without lifting a finger. If the winter is extremely cold, seed may not survive in the ground all year. Try to save a few by placing a piece of card or cloth around the plants when the seed starts to develop and catch the seeds as they fall.

Marigolds are an ideal container plant, and they tend to work well in sunny window boxes and in pots all round the garden. Marigolds will attract bees to herb gardens and vegetable plots. Place a large container or pot of marigold flowers in the middle of your plot to attract the eye and the good bugs!

Containers must be well-drained and plants should be watered regularly.

Eating marigolds

The bright orange marigold petals are a wonderful addition to all sorts of meals. Marigolds have been used to colour cheese in the past, and can be added to homemade cheeses to improve the colour and to add a little extra *je ne sais quoi* to your recipe. Marigolds are also used in bread making.

The marigold has long been considered a useful healing herb, as well as being employed in the kitchen usually in the form of a garnish. The leaves are also edible and can be added to salads, if you like the taste. Use only the young leaves.

Pick flowers just before you need them if possible, but always on the same day of eating. Gently pull apart the petals from the flower head and use them in the following ways:

- Stir carefully into a cold rice salad.
- Sprinkle into the salad bowl and stir in gently, or use as a garnish.
- Mix in to stir-fries after cooking.
- Stir into hot cooked rice to add the illusion of saffron!
- Sprinkle petals over chocolate or lemon cakes and gateaux.
- Garnish fruit salads and ice creams.

- Use the bright colours to add imagination and flair to everyday meals.

Whole blooms can be used to garnish:

- green or other mixed salads
- elaborate fruit desserts
- the dinner table. A single flower on side plates takes little effort but is very effective.

Marigold petals are a beautiful, bright orange colour and will compliment most food displays or individual dishes. Don't forget to use them. Small posies in vases or bowls add a touch of elegance to a dinner party.

NASTURTIUMS

About nasturtiums

Nasturtiums are a hardy, self-seeding herb that will cover a whole bed if not checked. Plant one or two nasturtium plants in the vegetable plot as they repel the bad insects and encourage the good guys! Little data is available about the properties of nasturtiums, although they are known to have a high vitamin C content. The flowers and leaves have a peppery taste similar to watercress.

Nasturtium flowers have been used as a culinary flower and herb for centuries. They are a trailing vine and can be grown as ground cover or trained to climb over a trellis to create a flowering fence or border. They are an attractive addition to a herb garden and can also be grown in pots on a patio or balcony.

The flowers, leaves and seeds can all be used in the kitchen and should be! Nasturtium seeds are a good substitute for the more expensive caper, which is an important pickling spice. Seed can be collected and stored for use in the kitchen or sown the following year.

Growing nasturtiums

Nasturtiums are classified as a herb and are probably one of the easiest plants to grow in your garden. They can be trained to climb fences or left as good ground cover. The foliage is fairly dense which helps to discourage weeds. It is a good plant to have in the vegetable garden, although it does tend to re-seed itself, and in areas where there hasn't been a heavy frost they are likely to come up on their own year after year. Don't feed the soil unless it is very poor. Nasturtiums will produce lots of leaf but little flower in very rich soil.

They can be started from seed early in the year. Fill well-drained trays or pots with potting compost, and plant two or three seeds per pot or thinly in a tray.

Nasturtiums grow quickly though and, rather than taking up valuable space in the greenhouse or conservatory with seed trays, it's just as good to wait a couple of months and sow directly outside.

Wait until all danger of frost has passed then dig over the ground and remove any perennial weeds or non-organic debris. Rake to a fine tilth. Then sow seeds 8–12 in (20–30 cm) apart. The seeds are large and easy to handle.

Fix up a trellis or some hooks on to a fence if you want the plants to climb. When they start to grow you will probably have to help them find their way but, once they get going, very little needs doing apart from making sure they get enough water.

With a little careful planning you may only ever have to buy one packet of nasturtium seeds. When the seeds start to appear on your plants, lay a sheet of card or cloth under the plants to collect them as they drop. Leave these seeds to dry indoors for a day then put them into a jar for sowing next year or using in the kitchen. In some areas, nasturtiums will re-seed themselves and come up year after year.

Nasturtiums are a good container plant. They do need a lot of water though so pots should never be allowed to dry out.

All containers and pots must be well drained.

Eating nasturtiums

There's a lot of food value in a nasturtium plant. The flowers, leaves and seed are all usable in the kitchen. The seeds can be used to replace capers in pickling spice.

PICKLING

Add nasturtium seeds to white wine vinegar and leave for a few weeks before using so that the flavour seeps into the vinegar. Seeds can be bruised or broken for a stronger or faster effect. The vinegar should be strained if broken seeds are used.

LEAVES

Nasturtium leaves can be shredded or chopped finely and added to:

- green salads. Toss into a bowl with mixed shredded lettuce, then add other ingredients. Nasturtium leaves have a peppery taste and should be used in moderation with milder tasting foods.
- stir-fries. Finely slice or chop the leaves and add to stir-fry ingredients in the last minute or two of the cooking time.

Leaves can also be chopped finely and used to garnish soups or other dishes.

FLOWERS

Nasturtium flowers make a very elegant garnish. They always add a touch of sophistication to a dinner table.

- Throw a few on top of a salad.
- Place a single flower on side plates.
- Arrange different coloured nasturtium flowers around a main dish just before serving.
- Use flowers to decorate a special occasion cake. Flowers taste peppery like the leaves so it may be advisable not to eat the flowers with a mouthful of cake!

And there's nothing to stop you livening up the taste buds while you are pottering in the garden! Young nasturtium leaves are very high in vitamin C and are a good food to pick and eat while wandering around the garden.

ROSES

About roses

There are over ten thousand different varieties of rose – many people make a lifetime study of this wonderful flower and spend years creating new varieties. What a magical job!

Most roses are edible and can be used in decorations and flavourings in the kitchen. The dog rose, often found growing wild, produces rose hips that contain more vitamin C gram for gram than oranges. The dog rose is a hardy plant and a useful one to grow now that many hedgerows have disappeared.

Rose hips were grown and collected during the war years and made into rose hip syrup, one of the most popular cordials around, as well as being a good source of vitamins, especially during those years when nutritious food was scarce. Many of us in the UK were brought up on rose hip syrup.

Roses are a passionate hobby for many people and there is always good advice to be found from local growers. They have been cultivated for over two thousand years and are known as the queen of flowers.

Growing roses

Roses can be started from seed but could take up to two years to germinate. They are usually propagated from cuttings. Rose trees of all varieties are available from most garden suppliers. Make sure your rose tree or shrub has recommended growing and planting instructions with it. Different varieties have different requirements.

Cuttings can be taken from an established plant. The best time to do this is at pruning time, after all the flowers have finished for the year. Trim your cuttings and only use the healthiest looking pieces. Cut them back to about 3 or 4 in (7–10 cm) and push them into pots of fresh compost. Water well after planting. Keep the soil damp but never too wet, and look after them until the cuttings have established roots and can be planted out into their permanent position.

Cuttings can be started in a seedbed but should be protected over the winter months with a cloche. Some cuttings may have developed roots the following spring but others may take a little longer.

New shoots are also used to propagate roses. Remove new shoots and plant them in fresh compost as with cuttings. Look after them until the roots have developed.

Dog roses are rambling plants and can be propagated by the layering method. Choose a healthy lower branch and push into the soil where it comfortably touches the ground. Secure with a V-shaped peg, cover with fresh compost then water. When the new plant has developed roots it can be cut from the mother plant and transplanted.

Roses are hardy woody plants and are generally easy to grow and maintain. Most rose varieties need pruning once a year. Take out any dead wood and overcrowding branches. Let the plant breathe.

Climbing roses can be trained to grow over any garden structure or on a fence or wall. Cut the plants back regularly to allow healthy growth and lots of flowers. Gently tie branches to hooks or weave them through trellises or other structures.

Check on manufacturer's growing recommendations for any further advice when buying hybrid varieties of rose. Grow a dog rose in a 'wild' part of the garden to bring a splash of colour and encourage bees and other wildlife to the garden. Although dog roses grow wild in some rural areas, it is a useful plant to grow and can be more or less left to its own devices.

As roses come in all shapes and sizes, a suitable variety for container growing will be easily found. Avoid the large rambling roses and stick to smaller bush varieties. Always use well-drained containers, water regularly, and feed from time to time if necessary.

Always check on manufacturer's growing recommendations when you buy your rose, or if you are using cuttings, check the mother plant. If it is thriving, copy the environment for your new plants.

Eating roses

Roses are considered to be a herb and are very practical to grow in the home garden. Apart from the single rose or extravagant bouquet gracing a dinner table, the leaves and fruits are also usable.

FLOWERS

Rose flowers are used to decorate gateaux and other desserts. Generally small roses, such as the tea rose, are used for decoration and can be frosted. To frost flowers, dip the top of the flower very gently into beaten egg white then into fine sugar. Leave to dry.

The petals can be scattered over large desserts or a couple of petals arranged on individual helpings. Rose petals are useful for flavouring food. Add petals to the blender when mixing ice creams or cakes.

LEAVES

Rose leaves make an enjoyable herbal tea. Pour boiling water on a few leaves in a jug. Cover and leave to infuse for about five minutes then strain and drink.

ROSE HIPS

Rose hips are the fruits of the rose plant and, gram for gram, are higher in vitamin C content than citrus fruits. Use them! Rose hips have been made into cordials for generations and can be added to homemade country wines.

Cut rosehips and remove the seeds, then simmer in a little water until soft. Mash and sieve or put through a blender. Use the remaining puree as a concentrate for:

- Making juices and wines. Add hot water and a little sugar and lemon juice if liked. Leave for a few minutes for the flavours to absorb before straining. Drink immediately or leave to cool and chill. For wines, rose hips can be added with the grapes or other fruit.
- Blending into ice cream or other desserts.

The combination of beautiful displays and useful flavourings puts roses in the 'must-grow' category in the garden!

HOUSEHOLD TIPS

- Add rose petals to pot pourri mixes for colour and scent.

VIOLETS

About violets

In some rural areas, wild violets can still be found at the right time of year. They flower in late winter or early spring but tend to be very shy, often growing well hidden amongst other wild flowers or grassland. Look out for them in the spring around your local parks and woodland. Once established, violets make good ground cover only growing to 3 or 4 in (7–10 cm) in height.

Violets have been cultivated as a medicinal herb for at least 2,500 years and are still used today in many herbal preparations across the world. The delicate flowers are candied and used to decorate celebration cakes and other desserts. Violets have a very distinct flavour and once tried can't be forgotten. The flowers and leaves are edible.

Violet leaves have expectorant qualities and can alleviate bronchial symptoms. They have also been found to aid in curing certain types of cancer. The flowers and leaves have mild laxative properties and therefore shouldn't be taken in large doses. Violets, being woodland plants, like a semi-shady position so will do well in a part of the garden where the sun doesn't shine all the time.

Growing violets

Growing violets from seed can be erratic at best but is possible. Seed should be started in well-drained pots or trays of fresh compost. The compost should be kept damp but not waterlogged. Germination can take some time. Although violets tolerate low temperatures, at this stage they need to be kept warm. Keep trays and pots in a warm conservatory or greenhouse, if possible, or in a warm bright place indoors. Check for any manufacturer's growing recommendations on the seed packet.

Keep warm and watered until seedlings are large enough to handle and all danger of frost has passed before planting out in their permanent position in the garden. Allow about 12 in (30 cm) of space between plants.

The quickest way to get a violet bed under way is to buy plants from your garden supplier or a local grower. *Viola odorata* is the species known as 'sweet violets' and is probably the best one to grow if possible.

Choose a fairly shady spot in the garden for your plants. They will grow in a sunny position but tend to dry out too quickly. Many flowering plants need a sunny spot so violets are an ideal plant to fill a shady area. They are a good ground cover and also flower early in the year before the summer blooms take over.

Dig over the ground before planting and remove any large stones, non-organic debris and perennial weeds.

In the autumn, new plants can be propagated from the old. There are three ways you can do this:

- Runners: Violets send out runners like strawberry plants and will replant themselves given the right conditions. Otherwise carefully remove plants from the main plant and re-plant somewhere else.
- Root division: Dig carefully around the plants, when they have finished flowering and lift them out of the ground. Separate the roots and re-plant pieces immediately into pots or containers until the following spring. Put them out in the garden when they are growing well.
- Cuttings: Take cuttings from healthy plants when they have finished flowering and push into pots of fresh compost. Keep indoors or protect from the cold during the winter. Plant out in the following autumn when the cuttings have developed roots.

Violet plants are evergreen and the leaves can be used all year round.

Violets are indigenous to woodland and part shady areas although given the right conditions, they may grow well in pots and containers. The plants do send out runners so the pots should be fairly large to accommodate these.

Use well-drained pots and water regularly but don't let the compost get too wet. Violets probably won't do well in full sun, so a little shade is needed.

Eating violets

Pick violets for use when they bloom. Pick them carefully so you don't pull up the whole plant. The flowering season doesn't last long so the more you grow the better. The leaves stay green all year and can be used anytime.

FLOWERS

Violet flowers can be used in the following ways.

- Add to salads. Toss gently into a green salad or use to garnish any mixed salad. The violet flowers colour the dish and add an extra special taste.
- Infuse to make tea. Simply pour boiling water over a few violets in a jug and leave to steep for five minutes. Strain and drink while still hot. Dried flowers can be used to make tea as well, so if you have too many to use in the spring dry a few for the winter months. Hang them upside down until crisp then gently put into jars and keep out of direct light.
- Crystallise to decorate celebration cakes and elaborate desserts. Or rather than going through the whole crystallising process, frost the flowers instead. Dip tips of flowers in beaten egg white then in sugar. Leave to dry before using.
- Scatter violets over a dinner table or collect small bunches and arrange them in elegant bowls or vases.

LEAVES

Leaves can be used to make tea and also for adding flavour to any dish that could 'do with a touch of violets'.

CHAPTER 7

THE STORE CUPBOARD

There are a number of simple ways to store your well-earned crops from the garden, as well as a few more complicated methods.

BOTTLING

Bottling fruit and vegetables is a worthwhile storage method if you have the right equipment and do it properly. Bottling fruit and veg requires a certain amount of care as bacteria can enter the food. Temperatures must be met and sterilising bottles and sealing them is imperative.

There are several different methods for bottling foods. For each method, use undamaged fruit or vegetables and prepare them by washing, draining, and then peeling and/or slicing.

The quickest way to bottle is to use a pressure cooker, although the cooker must be able to maintain a low pressure throughout the process.

Alternatively you can use a large saucepan with a false bottom or a wire rack at the bottom. Jars will crack if they are in direct contact with the saucepan when it is over the heat. Jars with rubber seals and spring clips should be used to keep your foods preserved well. The most useful ones have a capacity of 1 lb (500 g) or 2 lb (1 kg). All jars must be sterilised before using. You'll also need a decent thermometer to check that the correct temperature is reached.

Pack the prepared cold fruit or vegetables into jars. Pour over water, brine or fruit syrup so that the liquid fills all the gaps. Water can be used with all foods but you may choose to use brine for vegetables and syrup for fruit as you prefer. Place the jars in a saucepan of cold water. The water should be brought to the boil slowly and simmered until the correct temperature has been reached. Alternatively jars can be packed with warm fruit and water and placed in hot water to reduce the cooking time.

Bottling can also be done in a very slow oven. The jars must not touch each other or the sides of the oven.

Different foods require different cooking times and temperatures to kill bacteria and preserve them safely. Approximately 190.4°F or 88°C is the usual temperature required to bottle fruits and vegetables using a hot water saucepan method, although with a cold water process a slightly lower temperature will work. Cooking times vary between about 2 and 15 minutes, depending on the foods you are bottling. A pressure cooker will sort it all out in about one or two minutes. Check temperature and time charts for each type of food before processing. There is a very informative and useful section on the website www.allotment.org.uk – follow the information links.

Suitable foods for bottling

Most fruits and vegetables can be bottled or canned although certain foods lose some of their colour and texture during the bottling process. Generally most fruits are very suitable for bottling, as long as they are undamaged and prepared correctly. Some green vegetables will lose some colour and texture, but will stay perfectly edible.

PRESERVING

Although making jams, jellies and pickles is similar to bottling food, the process is less time consuming and, as you can make all sorts of jams and pickles, is far more fun than simply storing food in its original state. Most fruit and veg can be made into jams or pickles and there are only a few basic rules to follow for either preserving method.

Jams and jellies require sugar to preserve the fruit and generally pickled vegetables are preserved with vinegar.

Suitable foods for preserving

Soft fruits are perfect for making jams and jellies. See Chapter 5 for recipes for strawberry jam and others. Citrus fruits such as oranges and lemons can be made into marmalade, using the same basic principle as sweet fruit jams.

Apples and pears can be puréed and, after storing in jars, can be used to make pies and other dishes in the winter months. Apple purée or apple sauce can be served with a favourite roast pork dinner, or eaten as a dessert with ice cream. Children tend to like easy to eat foods and puréed fruit is a good way of getting them to eat a daily portion or two of fruit.

FREEZING

Freezing is probably the easiest and quickest way to preserve food, although not all foods will freeze and keep their texture and taste. With soft fruits, freezing quickly helps to keep the texture and flavour but inevitably some will be lost during freezing. One way round this is to make up whole dishes before freezing. For example a blackberry and apple pie may be more acceptable in its different texture than simply a bag of apples and blackberries.

Lay fruits, vegetables or herbs on trays and freeze quickly. Store in containers or bags and label before storing in the freezer.

Suitable foods for freezing

Most foods can be successfully frozen although fruit and veg with a high water content will dramatically change texture and, in some cases, colour, after freezing. Lettuce is very definitely a vegetable *not* to freeze, although, if frozen quickly, other leafy vegetables such as spinach will work reasonably well. Peas, beans, broccoli and cauliflower freeze successfully.

DRYING

Some food crops dry incredibly well, and it's a good idea to take advantage of this fact if you have storage space and lots of excess food from the garden. Always make sure food is properly dried before storing to avoid cross contamination or mould forming.

Suitable foods for drying

HERBS AND LEAFY VEGETABLES

Hang bunches of herbs, or single stems, in a dark dust-free place for up to a couple of weeks until completely dry. Some herbs will be dry enough in two or three days. Check regularly. Hang the herbs in paper bags to protect from dust and airborne mites. The bags will also collect any seeds or dried leaf that may fall from the stems or bunches. When completely dry, crumble and store the herbs in sealed glass jars and label. Keep the jars out of direct sunlight. Seeds can be kept for use in the kitchen or for sowing next year.

Most vegetables can be dried using a home food dryer or in a slow oven. Vegetables should be blanched first to kill any bugs. Slice or cut vegetables and place in a muslin or cheesecloth bag and place in a saucepan of boiling water. Keep the water boiling for about five minutes. Remove the bag from the saucepan and place in a bowl of cold water for five minutes. (This seals in the vitamins and minerals.) Drain well then spread a single layer of prepared vegetables on a rack in a home dryer or dry in a fairly cool oven, as described on page 186 for dried tomatoes.

PEAS AND BEANS

Peas and beans are exceptionally good for drying. Dried peas used to be taken on long sea voyages many years ago and would keep the crew and passengers fed for months. Dried peas and beans are simple to prepare and, as far as possible, should be left on the plant until totally mature and dry. Otherwise lay them on trays in a warm dry place until all trace of moisture is gone before storing.

Make sure there are no holes in peas and beans before storing as this can indicate that worms are present. Rather than picking over individual peas or beans to check for worms, fill a bowl with water and put the peas or beans in the water. The ones that float will have holes and should not be stored unless you are sure there is no worm left inside. These can be eaten but the worms will have eaten a lot of the goodness so try and store only the best, especially if you are likely to be keeping them for several months. They will keep almost indefinitely if prepared well and stored out of direct light in sealed jars.

MUSHROOMS

Mushrooms are a viable produce to dry. They can be strung together and hung over a range or radiator for a few days, then bagged and labelled before storing. Keep them out of direct light.

TOMATOES

Sun-dried tomatoes are a popular food but can be expensive to buy. Tomatoes can, however, be dried at home very successfully. Although they should be 'sun' dried, there is little chance of finding enough hours of sunshine in the UK at the end of the summer, but tomatoes can be dried successfully in a slow oven.

Cut tomatoes in half and place them cut side up on a baking sheet, leaving a little space between them. Put the tray in a very slow oven (Gas Mark ½, 250°F or 130°C) for an hour or two. Check every 30 minutes or so, and remove the tomatoes that are completely dry. If the tomatoes start to cook, leave the oven door ajar. At the end of this drying process, allow the tomatoes to cool completely and store in labelled bags or containers out of direct light. Sprinkle a little chopped basil, sea salt or even parmesan cheese if liked over the tomatoes before drying and store as above.

CHAPTER 8

GARDENING TIPS AND TRICKS

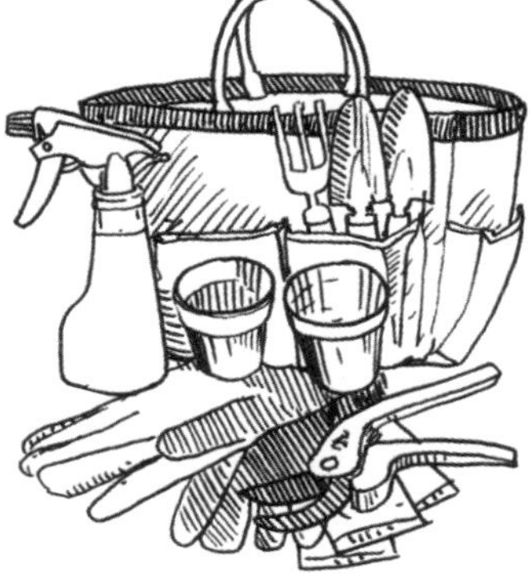

A little preparation goes a long way in the garden. Scattering the seed and hoping for the best won't produce the results you want. If you get to know your garden – the hot spots, the wet spots and any drafty areas – you can accommodate your plants well and get great results. Plants need water, light and air to thrive. Some need more of one and less of another, which is why good preparation will bring the best results as well as a garden that takes less time and effort in the long run to maintain.

Any neglected plants can be brought back to life with a little care and attention. Old rose trees and shrubs will benefit from a heavy pruning. Any plants that look well past their use-by date or don't fit in with your garden plans have to go. Dig them up and put them on the compost heap. Any diseased plants should be burned.

Are there areas of the garden that are magnets for local cats or other animals? A couple of paving slabs over a sandy area will put the local cat's bathroom out of action. Keeping grass cut short will also deter cats and other wildlife from damaging your plants. Very fine soil can be mulched until the feline population gets the message. If cats really are a nuisance in your garden, make sure you protect seeds with a cloche or cover straight after sowing.

PLANNING

Most plants thrive in sunlight, so the best place to put your shed will be in a shady spot in the garden. Don't waste a sunny position. Make sure you can clear right around the shed so that hedgerows or stray brambles don't grow over it.

The rest of the garden can be broken up with various beds, rockeries, water features, seating areas and children's play areas. Draw a plan of your garden. It doesn't have to be to scale, although a little precision is always useful!

Decide where your priorities lie in the garden. Consider some of these ideas:

- **Seating** can be placed among the herb beds or rose garden as well as on the patio. Consider a garden arbour with a seat. Grapes or other climbing vines can be grown over them, making the most of the space. Or build a bench around a tree – remember to allow room for the tree to grow though.
- **Containers of herbs and flowers** grace a patio and can also draw the eye to features around the garden. A large container of marigolds next to the back door brightens up the house and a container of flowering herbs will enhance a water feature.
- **Vegetable beds** in a *le potager* design makes the whole vegetable gardening thing seem a lot less overwhelming. Simply create small square beds where you can grow vegetables with herbs around the edges. Get creative with this idea. For example, bright green herbs around a bed of red cabbage look stunning.

- **Raised beds** need a lot less maintenance than a regular vegetable patch. They have to be narrow enough to reach the middle from both sides and then once dug over thoroughly, won't need digging again for a few years. These beds can be permanent and have brick or wooden sides, creating a feature of themselves in your garden. Higher beds are also useful for the physically challenged as they require less bending over or kneeling.

- **Flowers and herbs** can be mixed in with vegetable and fruit crops as long as they don't overcrowd. Herbs are good plants to grow with your vegetables as many of them are strong smelling and deter pests from vegetable crops. Flowers will encourage pollinating bees to your garden.

- A **water feature** is sometimes considered to be a luxury but a pond will encourage wildlife to your garden. Frogs and toads live happily in a lush vegetable garden with a pond nearby and they are the best organic slug repellent around. Ponds and water features also attract children, providing a perfect way to get them away from the latest computer game!

- A **compost heap** is essential if you are going to take your gardening seriously. Either build it or buy one of the composting tumblers available in big garden centres or suppliers. Composting rotten fruit and vegetables and peelings creates rich soil you can use every year to plant seedlings or container plants. This really is recycling at its best. Dig out the bottom of your compost heap once a year and sieve the soil before using it. A simple garden sieve can be made by stretching a piece of chicken wire across an old bottomless saucepan or strong bucket. A compost heap needs to be kept warm but it also needs air to break down the vegetation. Leave gaps in the sides for air and cover the top after adding composting material.

TOOLS

Once you have decided what you are doing and where everything is going, a few tools will come in handy. You won't need everything to begin with and quality is better than quantity every time when it comes to garden tools. Cheap tools can buckle and cause damage to your plants as well as to you.

To get your fruit, vegetable, herb or flowerbed started, you will need to buy:

- A **spade and fork** for digging over, breaking up the ground and edging. Both tools must be the right height for you to use them. Handle them in the shop before you buy. Make sure you don't have to lean over the handle or that it isn't too long for you. Weight is also important. If you can hardly lift it in the shop, you definitely won't be able to lift it when it's full of wet soil. A sharp edge on your spade is useful for defining your beds, which in turn helps to keep weeds from straying into them.
- A **rake and a hoe** are essential for breaking up the ground and levelling off. Rakes are also useful for dragging stones from the surface of the soil, so make sure it is strong. A hoe should be fairly sharp for cutting through soil. Both tools must be the right height and weight as above.
- A **hand trowel and watering can** are the only hand tools you will need to begin gardening. You can add more later as and when they are needed. The trowel must be strong and the watering can should have a rosette attachment. Make sure the can isn't too heavy for you; when it's full of water it will be a lot heavier!

For seed sowers a few extra bits and pieces are needed, although alternatives can be found:

POTS

- Plastic green or black pots can be bought in most garden suppliers and there are often biodegradable alternatives.
- Save yoghurt and dessert pots, wash and dry them thoroughly then carefully punch holes in the bottom for drainage. Don't use pots without holes as seeds will rot.
- Inner cardboard tubes from kitchen or toilet rolls make ideal seed starters. The whole tube or roll can be planted as they are biodegradable and, although they are made of card, they last a while and are ideal for seeds that are fairly quick to germinate such as tomatoes, lettuces and most other everyday vegetables. Cut each tube in half to get two pots for the price of one.
- Make pots from newspaper, using a specially designed pot maker, available in larger garden centres.

SEED TRAYS

- Buy a few seed trays from a garden centre but don't buy flimsy trays as they tend to crack and break easily.
- Old paint roller trays are a good alternative to bought seed trays. Make sure all paint is thoroughly washed away before filling with compost. Punch holes in the bottom for drainage.
- Deep silver foil baking dishes can also be used. They should be rinsed after using and holes punched in the bottom. The very shallow trays aren't really deep enough for most seedlings, although they are perfect for mustard and cress.

ROW MARKERS

- Plastic labels can be bought from garden suppliers as well as the right type of marker to write on them.

- Get the kids making drinking-straw flags for your pot markers. Sellotape or glue a plain piece of paper around one end of a drinking straw. Leave enough space to write on. Cut some straws in half for seed tray markers.

- Use wooden lolly sticks, or collect small twigs on your next woodland walk.

OTHER HELPFUL ODDS AND ENDS

- A dry box is useful for keeping your seeds in before sowing.

- Keep a pen available to label your plants and a journal if you are keeping one.

- A pair of gardening gloves saves a lot of wear and tear on your hands and nails.

- An old spoon or fork from the cutlery drawer can be useful for transplanting small plants.

SOIL PREPARATION

Drainage

It's worth doing a little research into the condition of the soil in your garden, although we don't have to get too technical. Generally it's important to have well-drained soil. There are very few plants that will survive in waterlogged soil so that's the first check to make. Whatever you are planning to grow, whether it's fruit, vegetables herbs or flowers, you will need well-drained soil.

- Incorporate some fine gravel or sand to alleviate any drainage problems.

- Consider building raised beds if the ground is very badly drained.

- Or use containers to plant your crops.

Nutrients

Generally fruit and vegetables will need fairly well-nourished soil. Some herbs and a few fruits and veg will tolerate poor soil but in general, the more nutrients in the soil, the more your vegetables will thrive. And of course the more nutritious your vegetables, the better for you.

- Dig in some well-rotted manure or rich compost into the soil before planting.
- For root crops, it's advisable to dig the fertilisers into the ground during the previous autumn before spring plantings. Un-rotted material will cause root crops to 'fork' and also may be too rich for some young plants.

Digging over

Once the soil is in the condition you are happy with, it will need digging over if you haven't done so already. Don't over-do the digging. It's tempting on the first sunny day of the year to go out there and dig a whole bed over in one day but that usually results in an aching back and being out of action for a week or two.

Take it a little at a time. Even if you only dig over a square metre a day, it's good enough. It's also much better for the spirit as well as the body. If you plan to dig over only a small part of the large vegetable patch, it doesn't seem like a chore.

Dig as deep as you can the first time, especially if the ground hasn't been used for a while. Remove large stones, non-organic debris and any perennial weeds. Compost the weeds, keep the stones for drainage and edging later on and dispose of any other rubbish. Keep the area tidied as you go along.

When the bed has been dug over, rake to a fine tilth and let it rest. Some gardeners like to cover the area with black plastic or other materials to discourage weeds. If you cover the ground, remove the covering a week or two before planting to aerate the soil. Break up the surface with a hoe if necessary.

Mulch

A mulch is useful in the winter to prevent frost damage. It also keeps the weeds down during the summer and helps to keep moisture in. Use grass clippings, straw or other organic materials. Never mulch too close to your plants or they will suffocate. Lay your mulching material around the plants to cover the soil. It only needs to be a few centimetres deep.

MAINTENANCE

If possible, a garden should be maintained on a daily basis. With bad weather and short days this is not always possible. During the winter months, try and do some of the maintenance there isn't time for in the summer. For example, fixing garden fences, catches on gates, shed doors that won't close. Tidying up these little jobs in the winter makes the spring and summer seasons in the garden so much easier and more enjoyable.

Pruning can also be done during the autumn to early spring. Cut back your fruit bushes, roses, trees and other shrubs. A few minutes spent here and there will provide much better crops or blooms the following year.

Plant trees and other hardy shrubs in the autumn to settle in before the following spring.

Clover lawns

Lawn specialists get frustrated with clover growing in the lawn as it is considered to be a weed. However, clover stays green all year and doesn't need cutting as often as grass does. It also encourages bees to your garden, so factor this in if you have children as bare feet could get stung.

Raised beds

As mentioned before, raised beds really do take the hard work out of spring planting. Double dig your bed in the first year and make sure it's not too wide so that you can reach to the middle from both sides. Don't walk over the bed once dug and you will only need to gently fork it over the following spring before planting.

Plants can be placed closer together in a raised bed, giving you more available growing space.

Paved areas

A few paving slabs can be useful in the garden. Be adventurous and place one in the middle of a flowerbed to make a plinth for a particularly attractive container full of herbs. Paving slabs are also useful for covering sandy areas, preventing local cats using your garden as their public convenience.

THEMES

Themed gardens need a little more planning but the effect can be spectacular.

- **Meadow and wildlife gardens** are becoming very popular but if you want to grow vegetables alongside you may have a lot of weeding to do. Consider growing meadow flowers in a small part of your garden next to a path to discourage trailing plants from taking over. Bees will be attracted to a wildlife garden and help to pollinate your vegetables.

- A **butterfly garden** planted out with flowers that particularly attract butterflies is a popular and fairly simple theme to create, but again remember the veggies. Cabbage white butterflies let loose on your cabbages will lay eggs on the underside of the leaves and, if not spotted in time, the resulting caterpillars can demolish crops almost overnight.

- **Colours** can be used as a theme – blue flowers in the spring, yellow in the summer and so on. Become an expert flower grower and you will be sought after in your area. Scan a few catalogues for ideas. There are some wonderfully coloured hybrid blooms on the market these days. Not all flowers are annual but bulbs, such as tulips, daffodils and crocuses, will last for many years and often reproduce themselves, making your display bigger and better every year.

- **Rose gardens** have always been a gardener's delight and can be added to every year. From very tiny tea roses to large rambling dog roses, the choice is huge. Again browse a few catalogues to see what's available and what will suit your garden. Climbing roses brighten up a bare brick wall over a few growing seasons and will last for many years.

- Your garden could be given over completely to growing **herbs**. Herbs can be grown in containers and are useful and aromatic plants to grow in your garden. Herbs are a subject in themselves and can provide not only wonderful flavourings for food but also many can be used as alternative medicines and even cosmetics. See Chapter 4 for more herb ideas.

- **Water features** can be stunning and soothing, as any feng shui enthusiast will tell you. A small courtyard will be transformed with a water feature and a few containers of herbs. Let your imagination loose on this one. Create a rock garden or a rockery and have water trickling over the rocks into a pond. Fish are good entertainment for the kids and you could grow some excellent watercress in the running water. Features like this will take a certain amount of planning and budget should be considered. Look around before you buy. You may find something that suits your space even better than your original idea.

Any outdoor space is an extension of your home and, with a little attention, it will delight and inspire everyone. Give it some thought before you begin. Be realistic about how much time, effort and money you are prepared to invest.

Taking on too much too soon in a garden becomes overwhelming and all too easily gets neglected. If you are facing a huge task, take it on a little at a time. Decide to get a vegetable bed going the first year, adding other features in subsequent years, as and when you have the time available.

Gardens are there to grow and your garden should always be 'a work in progress' and never actually finished!

RESOURCES AND FURTHER READING

MORE TITLES BY LINDA GRAY

Grow Your Own Pharmacy (Findhorn Press)

Grow Your Own Winter Food (New Holland Publishers)

Granny's Book of Good Old Fashioned Common Sense (Black & White Publishing)

Self-Sufficiency: Herbs and Spices (New Holland Publishers)

WEBSITES

Gardening and plants

www.flower-and-garden-tips.com

www.bbc.co.uk/gardening

www.botanical.com

www.gardenguides.com

www.garden.org (National Gardening Association)

Healthy living

www.5aday.nhs.uk

www.bbc.co.uk/health/healthy_living

www.nutrition.org.uk (British Nutrition Foundation)

www.thinkvegetables.co.uk

FURTHER READING

The Practical Gardening Encyclopaedia (Colour Library)

Complete Garden Manual (Collins)

INDEX

Some other titles from How To Books

STORING YOUR HOME GROWN FRUIT AND VEGETABLES

How to make your garden's bounty last all year round

PAUL PEACOCK

The job's not done when the harvest is gathered in. You have to make this bounty last all year through – until next year's crop replaces it. This book represents the next stage for the fruit and vegetable gardener. It explains how to store food in the traditional way and focuses on methods by which the grower can keep vegetables and fruit for long periods without altering their fundamental form or flavour. From clamping to dark room storage, drying to bottling, shelving to curing, this book shows you how to keep as much of your crop as you want for yourself.

ISBN 978-1-905862-54-2

MAKING YOUR OWN SKIN CARE PRODUCTS

How to create skin care applications for particular skin types

SALLY HORNSEY

If treated and nourished properly your skin will be healthy and glowing, making you feel good and look great. This book will guide you through creating your own personal range of skin care applications, tailored to your particular skin type – or any body else's. The products made use natural ingredients where possible, and throughout the book you will find details of the purpose and benefits of the ingredients used. You will also learn about ingredients that can be substituted so that you can adapt the recipes to suit your or others' needs.

ISBN 978-1-905862-68-9

COUNTRY SKILLS AND CRAFTS

How to use, barter or sell what you raise, grow and make

MAUREEN LITTLE AND CRAIG HUGHES

More and more people want to acquire a set of new skills or build on their existing knowledge of the wide range of traditional cottage industries and country crafts. And more people than ever are also relocating to the countryside in search of a relaxed and locally-aware way of life.

If you aspire to live a simpler, more sustainable and self-sufficient life, this book is for you. It will help you make your aspirations a reality, and will unearth and develop your rural lifestyle talents. You too can live well, have fun and generate some income at the same time, whatever your background or current ability.

ISBN 978-1-905862-67-2

THE BEE GARDEN

How to create or adapt a garden to attract and nurture bees

MAUREEN LITTLE

Bees play a vital and irreplaceable role in pollinating our flowers, fruits and vegetables. The more bees in your garden the healthier, more productive and more pleasant a place it will be. Yet bees are declining rapidly and many people, even if they do not wish to keep bees themselves, are asking what can be done on an individual basis to help the bee. This book is a response to that request. It will demonstrate in one accessible volume how each of us can play our part in providing a bee-friendly environment, no matter how much gardening space and/or time we may have.

ISBN 978-1-905862-59-7

CHICKENS, DUCKS AND BEES

A beginner's guide to keeping livestock in the garden.

PAUL PEACOCK

Chickens, ducks and bees are the most likely candidates for the first time livestock owner – especially if you live in a town or have only a small amount of land. The book is full of sound, practical advice and looks at exactly what you need to get you started: the equipment, housing, space and feed. Taking the breeds best suited for the smaller garden, town garden, or allotment, the responsible care and management of these animals is thoroughly covered in a friendly, approachable style with their welfare always in mind.

ISBN 978-1-905862-573

FRESH BREAD AND BAKES FROM YOUR BREAD MACHINE

SUE SIMKINS

If you are thinking of buying a bread machine; or maybe you already have one, greatly under-used, at home: then this is the book for you. In her usual easy going and accessible style, Mrs Simkins explains how a bread machine enables you to make gorgeous fresh bread in your own home: quickly and easily and on a regular basis. Apart from loaves of bread and a selection of tea-time cakes made entirely in the bread machine, Mrs Simkins guides you through using the machine for mixing dough to make your own buns, rolls and pizza bases to bake in the oven – and even covers making your own pasta.

ISBN 978-1-905862-71-9

How To Books are available through all good online and high street bookshops, or you can order direct from us through Grantham Book Services.

Tel: +44 (0)1476 541080
Fax: +44 (0)1476 541061
Email: orders@gbs.tbs-ltd.co.uk

Or via our website

www.howtobooks.co.uk

To order via any of these methods please quote the title(s) of the book(s) and your credit card number together with its expiry date.

For further information about our books and catalogue, please contact:

How To Books
Spring Hill House
Spring Hill Road
Begbroke
Oxford
OX5 1RX

Visit our web site at

www.howtobooks.co.uk

Or you can contact us by email at info@howtobooks.co.uk